AF572529

DWELLING

Heather C. Akerberg

DWELLING

Burning Deck, / Anyart, Providence

Acknowledgments:

An earlier version of *Dwelling* was published as an "e-chapbook" at www.durationpress.com. Single poems have appeared in *Aufgabe, Bed, Conundrum* and *Nebraska Review.*

Burning Deck is the literature program of Anyart: Contemporary Arts Center, a tax-exempt (501c3), non-profit organization.

Cover Art: Untitled lino block print by Shelly Akerberg.

© 2008 by Heather C. Akerberg
ISBN13: 978-1-886224-89-6 original paperback
ISBN13: 978-1-886224-90-2 limited signed edition

for Joan and Shelly

CONTENTS

My body, still too heavy with sleep to move, would endeavour to construe from the pattern of its tiredness the position of its various limbs, in order to deduce therefrom the direction of the wall, the location of the furniture, to piece together and give a name to the house in which it lay.

—Marcel Proust, *Swann's Way*

I

the thaw of
this

sound
obscures

a word

heavies lips
where

that pleasure

of wonderment

of whispers

as dwelling place.

cold against toepad brings a warm sensation. each bump of plaster a syllabic message turned on its side. transliterates a story only this body recognizes. that the leg's reach determines each line's length — once caressed turns to sound. which couples with context to make sense of. a correlation between orchards and the cedar waxwing's *sreee*. how the habitat fits its body, how the body loses its sense if extracted. its bearings found when the foot reaches out from beneath cover.

wall bares the weight of home.

before sleep the body's geometry brushes against surroundings — suitable to one this key unlocks. postcards from a museum trip, mirror shaped as apple, jar filled with ticket stubs — a loose index. assembled. resemblances match features to transient feeling in gut. turning-tossing. so the first home's memory, deteriorating as the body it informs. remnants of paper, twig, fibers — form a cup and dome, or nest. appears steadfast as the object of a photograph. hands can imitate. the double-windows on either side and dormer above, with imposing maple just to the left, a childhood bedroom cornflower-blue and to the right. altered perhaps by scale. this likeness effected through waxy, colorful lines. a residential program, the adult impression. a child to comfort. a foot then too reached, to touch. these thoughts abreast with. house sparrow *cheeping.* forgotten stories, traces on the surface unseen. imperceptible but by ridges in print. past as diaphanous scrim / private view.

memories chosen as memories. attraction. through color, the selection follows an arc. a bodily appearance, a living space, she. as now, cerulean, blue as then. as the blue jay's feathers contain no pigment but refracted sunrays cast this light. this affect of coloration propels her toward. similitude. that history depends on who is telling and what story they choose, that hue is story — an inheritance, that the tone beckons an earlier one, which recalls sprightly times now tenebrous from age.

exterior view:

the house shaped like others: front porch, windows on either side. each slat aged and shedding its paint. a corner lot. the color of my choice my room then. this too interfused — an attempt to collect me denied you. father, now that it gets confused.

which is right and which wrong conditioned as. a jay will aggressively defend its territory. home. to prove even a raider of nests claims its own.

she wants to leave behind but forgiveness does not necessitate. oblivion. when she sleeps at night. erasure of representation — a new figure put in ones place. some sort of searching in visual discourse to connect with. form, hers. perhaps all houses are drawn from nostalgia. to deny this established need. to be said to exist, is. the dependence of language on remembering. nudged awake, select and replot.

so that some times he loved me and others I asked too much.

a floor and ceiling

held apart by

demarcation of space

makes place
for memories

are there to
give it a name for

rattling with

the comfort of belongings

inversion the prescribed action — the box either open or closed as the contents are not the same. a body tailored to its habitat. and adjusts. the superlative of what keeps out of sight. desire: to be close to. this or that being the only choices which somehow seem to differ from. a forgotten corner. this puzzlement of language where thought determines something hidden where only. exterior view: offers no window into.

in spring,

> we hatched quail — incubated and turned on time. I looked on as sister's fingers gentle against the shells bolstered father's pride. chicken-wire structure where latched door and the coop with nests boxed from sight proved unsubstantial against.

as when the first key

turns up only rehearsed secrets to placate. second guessing. always wanting a red front door and her childhood bedroom floor. she tells this one many things but mostly about the grate as if a portal to a nether region from where creatures emerged and withdrew. like the stories we tell ourselves before dreamtime. and another inside deeper still.

as home is nothing but familiar things but nothing communicable. a symbolic gesture, *la maison*. why thrush somehow makes robin more interesting though documented as bird. a fractalic map, mind. exists in relation to other stories on the shelf. perhaps something discernable in a face. the prince and his clothes or. she noticed it upon. to guess a history and inevitably err. one coast mistaken for another.

subject as composite he thought her. legible text. some rhyme scheme to lend it recognition. could easily construct her past. guess which event came first. her, knee deep in snow, coming home from school, following her sister's footsteps. whose plumage of chestnut-red or pale blue eggs shall be labeled birdsong, a childhood metaphor for the reflection of light off bedspread and curtain softly through glass pane from. there can be seen the barren branches of winter grey.

memory locates reception with associations of home and concomitance of its doorways. passes from one to the other. she is recognizable though his brief view. midday. transitional space she sights. the glossy black mantle of a starling. distinct, something of posture. reciprocal of which comes quick like a birder notes field marks and is swift to classify. this entanglement forever present. movement from periphery to backlit and aglow. she is framed as. subordinate beyond the threshold, waits. he wouldn't, couldn't possibly. a spatial relationship suggests a clock might be more to keep time.

hours ran round the grandfather's face. my gaze shifted only the few feet between window and tic-toc of. puzzlement at arrival, father, yours. stumbling for reason, I. or cause experienced as not the only time.

goldenrod, its claw so vibrant as to be likened to a crayon. starling. perceptible in her form — past pulled to the surface by another's selection. in glossing one discerns the difference between reminded and remembered — its similarity to the crested myna. though a reproduction knowingly lacks the same quality of age.

open to embrace, walls sharpen their corners. from what is evidence he is always there but some capacity. not as she is. afraid. that instead of embellishing a distant train whistle blows the constructed silence of room and folds time, joins past here with.

paper-airplane. your hands sounded sand against paper. built-in drawers the lime of liquid in the tube of the spirit level used to determine the plane. building at the foundation. just as. father, I wanted you to know I too. and letters stopped.

words here join — her motives impressed. hinge. this one often uses the conditional tense to define. the quality or essence of a thing. to get near, to see closely, to listen where nothing is, touch comes first. the closet with high shelves and pull-string illuminated felt like a private kingdom. her confusion stated when faced with departure. the hanging clothes stood in for a forests' worth of trees. texture: saw dust. he is always already existent and absence reveals. her regret.

by home, shaped.

II

unlike some
this
is what
at first sight,

seen in another

the visible
not read.

every edge
guards
for the words
dictation given to

complexity
perhaps
its disguise.

the parts one never sees. he determines to cross. precipice. results in him found. to not only but look with words where fascination dispels between what is meant and seen. infinite directions. upon entrance, the difference is clear what should one and what not see. the space. this intention looms. turns over several times, she does, in her head.

stanza.

whose fever knows a necessary duration. or foyer.

the efficient dissection of place. room. for archways in succession cause uninterrupted flowing as a riverbank might its river. he traces the title of a book on the desk, hers. specific objects: each in this room. before nervous fingers might check the passage, she. an odd position as one standing on the other side of the train platform the tracks rattling, as a famous portrait returning your stare, as subject.

the line of a frame traveled, mossy hillsides resound with white — an oblique statement of morning. slopes beneath cover might its transparency reveal too much or the leg disappears below. blueness of veins pierce through a cautionary tale. an injustice to prematurely assign sex with a pronoun. surely assumptions taint the view. like a dollhouse features unimposing and small. reclining with hands tucked under pillow. forming the soft shape of a lowercase *m* — melting. a woman's hips. a home, a wooden frame. shadows pale as this hour. the body materializes at the point just past its unraveling.

titanium white refers to fresh snow or this morning's light. no matter if it faces east or the angle of his relation, the consistent occurrence. windowpane. it resembles a dandelion puffed, if glow has a texture, and expresses fragility, his. languid or is. none too much different from the fables we tell ourselves. gently. ripples distort. like photo developing solution, skin hints at transformations below. that it is specific only to morning, that it is potent and miscible, that it expresses the difference between sleep and consciousness, is freely admitted. the rise of day. one looks in only to see oneself looking back.

today provides a propitious morning encounter with. greetings from the mockingbird, a story for her, hopping just atop a light-post. she might bite at her tongue — to save morality for a more human conversation. a varied song which alludes memory. this he'd rather silence the rule. of or pertaining to the mouth will prefer.

tomorrow weighs and measures to couple with intuition: nominalism or taxonomy. lose form when deprived of color. his negation of. displays the greatest truth of something without language, as *nada*. being dull in feather as most females of the species. her eyes nestle every bend, his face. devotion for each detail to classification of. a tactility not without merit. she believes. a tentative taste produced by sleight of hand, his. distrust followed by.

the appearance of a body approaching. curio cabinet: glass and reflection with an oak wood frame. a collector of sense data. the forming shape edges suggest. a living room. she walks across the floor naked. each shelf displays mementos and dust. her mouth moves, she says something when. now anywhere, she could be walking. say she is now standing beyond home in the private space. warm stomach. lulling. some sort of hypnotic pleasure, written. there in her hand — invisible foreign sky with cumulus clouds materializing.

reading: a subject is announced, she, and then another, he. a formed bridge like so. a plume of white just below blue wings, which are but reflected light. a color, a lone trumpet. walks across the living room. hand touches belly, its own. the salty scent of pacific blue demonstrative of. her difficulty in separating the texture from its briny taste. a body's weight sinking sounds like.

the sound

a mournful *coo*

gives it away

like a squeaky caster
though
one might mistake
while in-flight

the white-tipped feathers

for that of a blue jay
though

dovetail
joins here with

an initial intersection — loose for containing possibility. and she is out here in the living room, where alone she is with nothing to hold. the explanation of reasonable confidence corners don't allow. realized as wasted space only realized when two give up into functionality. the reason ground foragers eat crawling insects. let's say what is going to happen is known before — a story written and retold time again: he is always already gone, as expectation, hers. the reason disappointment does not discount the impetus. so it is. the illusive *chipping* so rarely heard. and always is avoided where this point.

he is not hopeful and she hopes for that to change. instinctive behavior. exactly why they sometimes rely on thick brush for cover. or an object. or a thing. or stuff. interjects silently but with grandeur. due to autumn migration, the denial of roost or any settling term, this sparrow. a mouth, missing, is really where disappointment arises or the eminent absence of what almost.

to wit: penetration — unlike some public proclaim. chiseling stone. he certainly dissuades her from a steady hand. this bad faith noted in swollen or broken chirography. forefinger. it means nothing being *non-* of what this would be normally. spoke and determined intermediate. scripted as a couch scene complete with street sounds and ceramic birds. is he solely diverted. every edge of the bric-a-brac unmissed by impatient fingers. battlements crumble. here witticisms serve as supple guards to what is deposed. to thoroughly pass through she wants but fails. to recognize her success. foreshadows an honest question. shoulders turned in like a willow branch bending. quietly *chirruping.* perhaps private is better suited but with addition arises bafflement. the difference between. he duly notes the complexity. cat's cradle. the size of which does not determine its strength or crenellation. when two with novelty as disguise.

a different knowing
could be cloaked

or her eyes were shut
though she knew

where the light fell

around the room
or perhaps the obvious

to decipher
the shape
of sound

the movement, as mouth
of a word
requires a history
with the language

or past experience of

silence proves dangerous where idleness takes possession. let's say a pedestal table topped with a crisp doily and a decorative vase. chipped. imperfect but grasping tightly to its seldom necessity. a line of reason she has. as abstract gives one a glimpse of mind, thinking. as she thinks. as a reader. the silent path of description leads to. how charming. a plywood front, no matter of ornament, does not make a home, to hold things, for nurturing, as family, to keep one near. this being a prerequisite for.

III

out of common
pitch
breaks
a whisper
she sometimes

wonders
at birdsong

inasmuch as

the heart
of home found

in sound
of this

preferring the prim path — an elusive position, theirs. upon entrance a room has a certain duration. a starting point and time. what shall be is determined as such. while doors suggest some opening she cannot look past. the chosen shape generally a pitched roof set atop. to rebuild what was once and now. which is this. space between a sweet erasure and some contrary circumstance he questions. either presupposition or nevermind. she, outside, does not equate to inside, though there might be more than the other choice. stillness which arises out of something once temporary, a house where the walls waver with. spatial memory.

fear out of aberration: a common calling. off come the gloves. she speaks in order that whoever is qualified. but more what she avoids. a glass and a question of volume. frozen with waiting that a pitch might be reached to shatter. brittle breaks. they are in a room together, recalled separately. for her, years passed before some tenderness. called by a name unfamiliar a previous version lacking accuracy. he whispers too much. white and oak wood floors supply a comfort associated with freedom from on-lookers. supple yields. perhaps she does not need to speak. or rather. sometimes is not the answer says he.

glossolalia is

glossolalia is garrulous is purposeless.

not now. walls define this space — though soundproof, striking the material. so he inasmuch as certain garments are restrictive. *en garde*. choking on a well-crafted *-ism* aged to perfect defense. she states an inventory of the room: a red velvet chair, a steel amorphous paper weight in the center of a glass coffee table, three windows, early evening light and her desires. a state of plunder, his. intersecting the floor's grain the windowpane stretches out shadowly. brown tones and play of light. he loosens his collar. hushed breath. she prepares to speak and does. braced for the quake imaginary she closes her eyes tight and grips her ears. in mind a sonorous moment. music box. this room allows the sound to come out: her succumbing. the wake of this rapture disproves.

some knowledge of
a place

or wonderment
for tactile distance

precedes a moving toward
the deliberate roundabout

description
of sense data

private and

fragile painted ceramic

innuendo
a better fit for most

misunderstanding happens at close range, vision foreshortened. the kitchen table is round: as suits this vernacular: is where they sit. it seems one might move closer. the illusion of proximity. aiming toward purposefulness — a residential program. the window draws her eyes which have no comfortable place to. crestfall. a fissure runs the diameter of the table — a battle line. respectfully to topple the hierarchy of this dwelling. he is both where she comes from and there. various strategies attempt to unsettle this history. something old / when it was new. might this impulse realized only in hindsight. the journey and its traveler. yielding that the erratic flight pattern of a bumble, unraveling. only later to recall this moment as when displeasure curbed by reflex as smile. his or hers. once again. their lips. immediate. the way ripe means soft. and nothing settled.

each has their own causality — building something unique using the same elements. once inside becomes apparent — outside only consists of the negative space left by this structure. there is the skin to consider not itself impenetrable though aiming for. that appearance and colors make memory last, that memory determines its own truth, that scale differs from his, hers.

father, is it the wrong thing or nothing at all. you said. to construct a stable structure set the brace diagonally, at 45°. what I so wanted to know, to delay even further. what was built lasted longer than.

the idea of smoke replaced by smokiness. there being no other creation but to think. doorbell. when it becomes impossible to differentiate building from cross-section. one may choose to stand back. when might home multiple its characteristics so as to be homey.

object contains within it — the finding of some feeling of. identification of which relies solely on imagination. that some things will not be thrown out, that a phrase might make her soften, that there are some things of which she is sure: she is uncertain, the possibility in him, several categories of value. malcontent — dysarthric heart. and so she seeks. this her steadfast position.

more alike than. you would know this as the one time.
otherwise the same, father. to you I keep running in.

to have feelings, not stupidity but poor judgment, for this one. recognized as her weakness. only wishes she could formulate some argument against her behaving. within the home each has purpose relating to history and function. precedential knowledge of. the privative element, he. being of value and the object just out of reach.

such things
cannot be made easy

as figure of speech
father
as narrative

whose color dull from age
while a germ
struggles for actuality

a medium of history

cumbrous

but relinquishable

as body is not so

by rote: the image of some shape present. a row of flats — approximating one another. her surface quality the same as before while her content varies. as change. he tells her. in this room where voices have before. emotional cacology. her possessive.

kept inside. the color of carpet, quality of light. going in. that there was blue-green carpet, that we had fish, the fabric of the chair synthetic against my skin, the weary milk box on the front steps. to remember how it was. the door offers little but at front a small window to look out. montage of seasons' lights held by memorypaste.

framed — a portrait — like an innocent man caught by chance at a moment captured in a photo now curled at the edges and discovered in a wooden box among more of the forgotten. as some life quantifiably collected and categorized. definitude creates definitude. might she unchart fate.

once now twice distilled, they. identical capacity misled by mass per unit. they as different which is just the same. revealed as.

> father, the way child-weight on your back solid beneath my small feet walking the path of your spine. wobbly. the hand you're dealt which you might be surprised at my remembering. these things cannot be made easy.

her experience her topic. marred. politics his choice. which are the same though slightly removed. one stands in for another or man or just something of him. for each. resignation and the tranquility that follows.

going against an ideal more of a resistance to. convention: that she would do the cooking, that he would take out the trash, that they might settle down, is one way. a varied song repeats a theme. rips open each, wants, and they stand divested. so believe they. being there only a moment that forces are in balance. dangerous to feel desire as dangerous to be. the affirmation felt. when the gifts that it seemed to coffer fade with the feeling. as whispers. the omissions she will soon execute. house now distorted as. the memories it holds.

IV

pitched relies

on what to either side of

its inclination
denotes

mnemonic cathedral

a dwelling
shaped by

its prescribed action

even as some
thing or one

of the elements

goes missing

one returns to the line's beginning, a yearly migration about a return. to a sandbar, a sedge meadow, a corn field. identity manifest through choice read. here as the corn poppy — precisely because of specificity. each sight. the curves and patches of a red — transliteration of its animating force. or warm memory sensate. each call a rattling *ka-roo*. there is she because she lives there. is another body or sound with. meaning is a skeleton with skin. weather-beaten timber exposed beneath exterior paint, chipped. that its every inch contains story, like her first baby tooth left in a glass of water for the tooth fairy, who paid her in change, a small fortune, that it shelters but is more than a place to hide, that though it seems consistent it feels different every day. sandhill crane. its silhouette the fascination of. something obeisant in each shift perhaps due to its backdrop. being the sky.

this room has a certain shape dissimilar from her body breathing just the same. leg reaches out for cold familiar. the shape, enduring simplicity, of the thing, a family, it, a house, is meant to hold. it is generally the shape of a thing. the program impresses domesticity — enshrined here. life within. makes a sound of settling.

each is unique not because of position or sex. that of superior structure being iron and labeled iron worker. father, I dreamt about you. one encourages its dissolve or waking. or two years since. bristly voice and gravelly chin. the slamming of screen door making it clear to be seen — everything through its hatch marks. I-beam resembles its name. having rigid edges and an impervious nature.

denying nostalgia. because she cannot see herself. the fog of morning does not keep her from apprehension. sensations being solitary. a window and a door for the possibility of public exposure — the walls' decorations as such. superlative of what keeps hidden. familiarity of which necessitates a blind knowing as if each object connects to her with a fine silk filament. glistening. the vanishing point, she, in this perspective.

place as both internal and external cue. family photos forgetting most. each string of sound, of smell, of weather woven into landscape. when she returns home is already. tree swallow's nest. whose closeness distinct as a steel chair's cold against her back like a stranger. if they would venture farther.

I lay in the grass. each blade meticulously plucked by fingers and placed to cover. it took hours. one was silent. I was still. until the green cradle materialized, molded by my shape. forever the building sequence guided by this artifact's completed state. weighs heavy. a structure considerably larger than its extrinsic influences. *locus classicus* of love — as this that is held.

a distant cry or past wonderment wants presence.

of form beyond memory shaped.

the hand if given

not in half-measures

concentrates or
is wide and full
with curiosity

the mouth has limitations
a pattern of sounds

a landscape
that wilts as

a graceful line

that merits circumspection

there is comfort in distraction. meadowlark. she stands at the window which is a wall. terrain where no other view offered captivates with habituation, hers. if there is water close, it makes itself known by song. the buff light through the trees refracted through glass blankets her face. rustling. not something one would choose to share.

skin neither partitive nor crystalline here further. I had a story to tell. whether outside pervaded in or whether a deaf ear was turned; no use for padlocks where the senses solicit no hold. father, no longer bothered.

that it is obviously raining or has. given any beginning she hypothesizes. a looking forward and away. rain imbues the soil, couples with streams, makes its way to the sea. an empty house and the possibility of guests. and from the field she hears a recognizable *tootling*. the most exterior of senses dematerialization of wall — when a wall is not a wall but a monotonous repeat. fingertips might hear something different emerge. it's best when it comes without force of thought.

> that upon meeting I kissed his cheek, that it left its imprint, that he was left with no way to respond. our discourse — a circuitous route. inside adopting the vastness of outside as another's eyes, the point of entrance. walking the labyrinth interchangeable with a euphemism for intimacy. a great fear.

maintaining inwardness. cuckoo or moonflower. when tangled things become a nest using items from the immediate vicinity. the other side of compulsory action. to build. grasp allows a bodily understanding of. traces on walls: something left behind: of sometime.

what categorizes space being prescribed action — allows digression. which each unit joins to form. wall. giving nothing more than its function. space implies perimeters — begins with a corner. might something be inscribed there with some feeling attached. she feels. and he. learned language of the senses: the trouble with describing things that are not said. because he never heard the sweet center of what was spoke, because she wished he had, because he knew the results.

as when push of breath finds the word. always falling short of. whippoorwill. meaning the word or its song.

its prescribed

action. departing from convention suggests some tradition. how birdsong the source of man's own music. as shelter has a history she thinks. built line by line or some minimum complete utterance. negating proclamation as one's desire. timbre better suited for. that poetic function comes first, that mind ascribes memory to each, that desire weakens, why she plans to place all photos of him in a box prescribed for.

may well rise upward as is its inclination. contained in the alveoli of. now tends to consolidate in a manner of honeycomb that denotes both its ambulatory arcade and its clerestory. a mnemonic cathedral. her verticality is one thing. to be sure she is standing, with hand, palm flat, on wall, a support, when it comes which is of no consequence to. a recountal.

wherein

cedar fashioned with dust and sharp incline this scent of found only on the stairs that lead to the attic of my. diaphanous. a body of articles: crayons, dictionary, sewing tin. fear of the dark. smaller hands. purpose no more than the curve of that ear. hushed-tones, motherly, drift to where I around the corner and determined. dim light from the window at top. the shape of the thing determines its ability to support, father. mingled for a moment with the season.

this instinct to inhabit fed

equally by that to construct. housed, not because living is the same or remembering. which may have identical rates of evaporation.

to find
the word
itself

cannot touch
the object

described as such

cupped between two hands
makes
sense origins

of whisper in ear
breath caught by fine filaments

send tingling

at the moment

recollected

anxiously the skyline whose lights mimic those once seen from the window of a cornflower-blue room where now the season expresses the basis for her returning for which she feels her mood colored by the ceiling at which she is staring while considering the possibility that home by definition is haunted.

she knows memory has to live somewhere. hummingbird. where some is the same location as. this varies accordingly though it seems unmoving the objects might. cartography of this is the place that she calls home. simply. points plotted: one nine inches directly above her navel, one 45° to the left. the fluttering of wings quicker than. here there. this point is always outside while always already being inside this. how some is more than the objects of which it consists: each cold plaster syllable against warm skin, the double-beat of the side-door swooshing shut, the specific scent of dusty corners.

these too or evolution decides the suitable shape and fate the finding.

Born and raised in the Midwest, Heather C. Akerberg resides in Omaha, Nebraska. She has taught English composition, creative writing and bookmaking, as well as cognitive skills. Heather is a freelance writer and sustainable agriculture enthusiast. She has an M.F.A. in Creative Writing from Brown University and a B.A. from the Jack Kerouac School at Naropa University. Her poetry has appeared in magazines like *Bombay Gin, Aufgabe, untitled* and *The Nebraska Review. Dwelling* is her first book.

This book was designed and computer typeset by Rosmarie Waldrop in 10 pt. Palatino. Printed on 55 lb. Writers' Natural (an acid-free paper), smyth-sewn and glued into paper covers by McNaughton & Gunn in Saline, Michigan. The cover uses an untitled lino block print by Shelly Akerberg. There are 1000 copies, of which 50 are numbered & signed.

20898

USMLE STEP 1

10

WITHDRAWN

IMMUNOLOGY

for the Boards and Wards

AF572554

BOLDERO LIBRARY
UCM
SCHOOL OF MEDICINE

Other books in the Boards and Wards series:

Boards & Wards—USMLE Steps 2 and 3
Pathophysiology for the Boards & Wards—USMLE Step 1
Dermatology for the Boards & Wards—USMLE Steps 1, 2, and 3
Microbiology for the Boards & Wards—USMLE Step 1
Ophthalmology/ENT for the Boards & Wards—USMLE Steps 1, 2, and 3
Behavioral Sciences and Outpatient Medicine for the Boards & Wards—USMLE Steps 1, 2, and 3

Notice: The indications and dosages of all drugs in this book have been recommended in the medical literature and conform to the practices of the general community. The medications described do not necessarily have specific approval by the Food and Drug Administration for use in the diseases and dosages for which they are recommended. The package insert for each drug should be consulted for use and dosage as approved by the FDA. Because standards for usage change, it is advisable to keep abreast of revised recommendations, particularly those concerning new drugs.

USMLE STEP 1

IMMUNOLOGY for the Boards and Wards

Carlos Ayala, MD
Clinical Fellow in Otology and Laryngology
Harvard Medical School
Resident in Otolaryngology
Harvard Otolaryngology Residency Program
Boston, Massachussetts

Brad Spellberg, MD
Resident in Internal Medicine
Harbor-UCLA Medical Center
Torrance, California

Blackwell Science

©2001 by Carlos Ayala and Brad Spellberg

BLACKWELL SCIENCE, INC.

Editorial Offices:

Commerce Place, 350 Main Street, Malden, Massachusetts 02148, USA
Osney Mead, Oxford OX2 0EL, England
25 John Street, London WC1N 2BL, England
23 Ainslie Place, Edinburgh EH3 6AJ, Scotland
54 University Street, Carlton, Victoria 3053, Australia

Other Editorial Offices:

Blackwell Wissenschafts-Verlag GmbH, Kurfürstendamm 57, 10707 Berlin, Germany
Blackwell Science KK, MG Kodenmacho Building, 7-10 Kodenmacho Nihonbashi, Chuo-ku, Tokyo 104, Japan
Iowa State University Press, A Blackwell Science Company, 2121 S. State Avenue, Ames, Iowa 50014-8300, USA

Distributors:

USA
Blackwell Science, Inc.
Commerce Place
350 Main Street
Malden, Massachusetts 02148
(Telephone orders: 800-215-1000 or 781-388-8250; fax orders: 781-388-8270)

Canada
Login Brothers Book Company
324 Saulteaux Crescent
Winnipeg, Manitoba R3J 3T2
(Telephone orders: 204-837-2987)

Australia
Blackwell Science Pty, Ltd.
54 University Street
Carlton, Victoria 3053
(Telephone orders: 03-9347-0300; fax orders: 03-9349-3016)

Outside North America and Australia
Blackwell Science, Ltd.
c/o Marston Book Services, Ltd.
P.O. Box 269
Abingdon
Oxon OX14 4YN
England
(Telephone orders: 44-01235-465500; fax orders: 44-01235-465555)

All rights reserved. No part of this book may be reproduced in any form or by any electronic or mechanical means, including information storage and retrieval systems, without permission in writing from the publisher, except by a reviewer who may quote brief passages in a review.

Acquisitions: Beverly Copland
Development: Julia Casson
Production: Shawn Girsberger
Manufacturing: Lisa Flanagan
Marketing Manager: Toni Fournier
Printed and bound by Capital City Press

Printed in the United States of America
01 02 03 04 5 4 3 2 1

The Blackwell Science logo is a trade mark of Blackwell Science Ltd., registered at the United Kingdom Trade Marks Registry

Library of Congress Cataloging-in-Publication Data

Ayala, Carlos, MD.
Immunology for the boards & wards / by Carlos Ayala and Brad Spellberg.
p.; cm.
ISBN 0-632-04574-4
1. Immunology. I. Title: Immunology for the boards and wards. II. Spellberg, Brad. III. Title.
[DNLM: 1. Immunity—physiology—Examination Questions. 2. Immune System—physiology—Examination Questions. QW 518.2 A973i 2001]
QR181 .A98 2001
616.07'9'076—dc21

00-066773

TABLE OF CONTENTS

TABLES

ABBREVIATIONS

↑ / ↓	increases or high/decreases or low
→	causes/leads to/analysis shows
dz	disease
1°/2°	primary/secondary
Ig	immunoglobulin
IL	interleukin
infxn	infection
µg/µl	microgram/microliter
pt(s)	patient(s)
Tx	Treatment
WBC	white blood cell

PREFACE

A number of medical students have told us they learned their immunology from the brief Appendix in our USMLE Step 1 review book, *Pathophysiology for the Boards and Wards*. With this in mind, we decided to expand the review section from our Step 1 book and develop it into a comprehensive overview of immunology geared towards clinicians.

In this text we view the immune system from the perspective of a host organism assigned the task of defending itself from a hostile, microbe-infested environment. Our book focuses on what really happens inside the body during an infection, from the assigned duties of each of the types of immune cells, to the arsenals they have at their disposal, to the cooperative defensive structures of immune organs and tissues. As per our usual style, the book is a broad overview but lacks excessive detail, making it perfect for busy students and housestaff preparing for the USMLE exams.

I. WHITE BLOOD CELLS (LEUKOCYTES)

A. Myeloid Cells

1. Granulocytes
   a. Neutrophils
      1) Most numerous WBCs (40–70% of total), short-lived (lifespan = 6–12 hrs)
      2) Neutrophil production in the bone marrow is stimulated by **granulocyte-colony stimulating factor** (G–CSF = Neupogen®), which is used clinically for neutropenia
      3) Neutrophils contain two types of cytoplasmic granules
         a) Primary granules contain small **cationic proteins called defensins**, which are inherently toxic to microbes, as well as the enzyme **myeloperoxidase**, which kills microbes via generation of hypochloric acid
         b) Secondary granules contain iron chelators and degradative enzymes
      4) Like all phagocytes, **neutrophils are intrinsically non-specific and without memory,** however like all phagocytes they are capable of **antibody-dependent cell-mediated cytotoxicity (ADCC)** (see Figure 1)

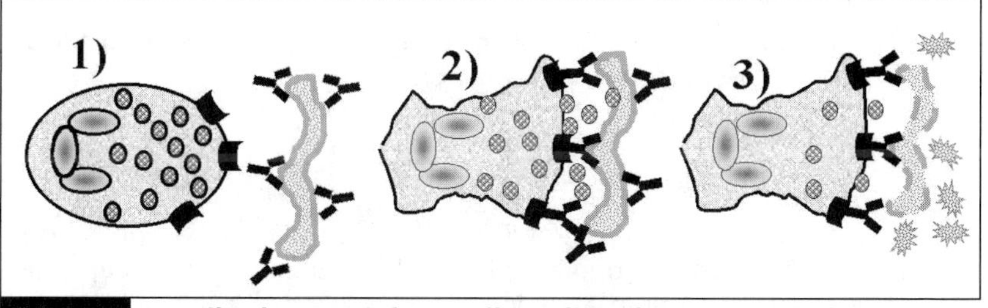

FIGURE 1 Antibody-Dependent Cell-Mediated Cytotoxicity (ADCC)

1) A leukocyte expressing receptors for the constant region of antibodies (Fcγ receptors) approaches a microbe (a hyphal fungus in this example) opsonized by serum antibodies. 2) Binding of opsonizing antibodies to the antibody-receptors on the leukocyte causes "capping," a phenomenon in which the leukocyte shifts its cytoplasm towards the bound microbe, followed by exocytosis of toxic granules in a directed fashion at the microbe. 3) Toxic granules punch holes in the microbial cell membrane and disrupt intracellular metabolism, resulting in microbial death. Note that the antigen specificity of ADCC is provided by the opsonizing antibody, not the leukocyte, which can bind to any antibody opsonizing any antigen.

BOLDERO LIBRARY

a) ADCC is when a phagocyte binds to the Fc (constant) portion of an antibody that is attached by its variable region to a microbe

b) The antibody thus provides **specificity** to a non-specific leukocyte, enabling it to target lytic enzyme secretions to the bound microbe

5) Dead neutrophils comprise pus

b. Eosinophils

1) **Play a role in parasitic defense,** utilizing IgE-dependent ADCC to secrete special anti-eukaryotic toxins onto parasites

2) Involved in asthma/allergy via IgE-provided antigen specificity

3) Differential diagnosis of peripheral eosinophilia (defined as 500 eosinophils/μl): the **NAACP mnemonic**

a) **N**eoplasm (often leukemia/lymphoma)/***N**ocardia*

b) **A**llergy/**A**sthma/**A**topy

c) ***A**spergillus* infections/**A**ddison's disease

d) **C**ollagen-Vascular dz/***C**occidioides*

e) **P**arasitic infections

c. Basophils

1) Rare cells (<1% of total), bind to IgE Fc region

2) Regulate vascular tone, can effect IgE-mediated Type I Hypersensitivity (see below)

d. Mast Cells

1) Tissue cells, not typically found in the blood

2) A myeloid cell of SEPARATE lineage from basophils (contrary to popular opinion, these ARE NOT tissue basophils: see Agis et al., J. Immunology 1993; 151:4221-4227)

3) **Responsible for IgE-mediated Type I Hypersensitivity**

2. Mononuclear Cells

a. Monocytes

1) Comprise 1–10% of WBCs, long-lived cells

2) Circulate in blood, eventually extravasate into tissues to become macrophages

b. Macrophages

   1) The terminally differentiated form of monocytes

   2) **These are the most phagocytic cells in the body**

   3) Are massive factories for cytokine production

   4) Destroy senescent RBCs in spleen and other tissues

   5) Act as professional Antigen Presenting Cells (APCs)

      a) **Professional APCs express Class II Major Histocompatibility Complex (MHC)**

      b) Class II MHC molecules allow professional APCs to present antigen to T-helper cells

3. Megakaryocytes

   a. Multinucleated giant cells (**the only polyploid cells in the body**)

   b. Have up to 32 or 64 times the normal cell DNA content

   c. Formed by precursors undergoing repeated DNA replication without cell division

   d. Act as factories which produce platelets by cell membrane budding

   e. Platelets secrete potent antimicrobial peptides similar to defensins

4. Dendritic Cells

   a. Not found in blood at high levels

   b. **The most efficient APCs in the body** (less phagocytic than macrophages but more efficient at antigen presentation due to more efficient co-stimulation of T cells)

   c. Reside in epithelial and lymph tissues most of the time—**Langerhans cells are a special population of dendritic cells found in the skin**

   d. Dendritic cells sample their environments by phagocytosing antigen

   e. After taking up antigen, dendritic cells migrate via vasculature to the spleen or via lymph channels to lymph nodes, and initiate immune responses by activating T cells

B. Lymphoid Cells

1. B Lymphocytes
   a. **Identifiable by surface expression of antibody, which serves as the B cell receptor**
      1) **Antibodies are tetramers composed of two identical heavy chain molecules and two identical light chain molecules** (see Figure 2)
      2) **Both heavy and light chain molecules have constant regions and variable regions**
         a) Constant regions of heavy chains come in one of five varieties, defining the antibody subtype: IgM, IgD, IgG, IgE, and IgA (see Table 1) (**Mnemonic:** **M**edical **D**octors **G**ive **E**veryone **A**spirin)

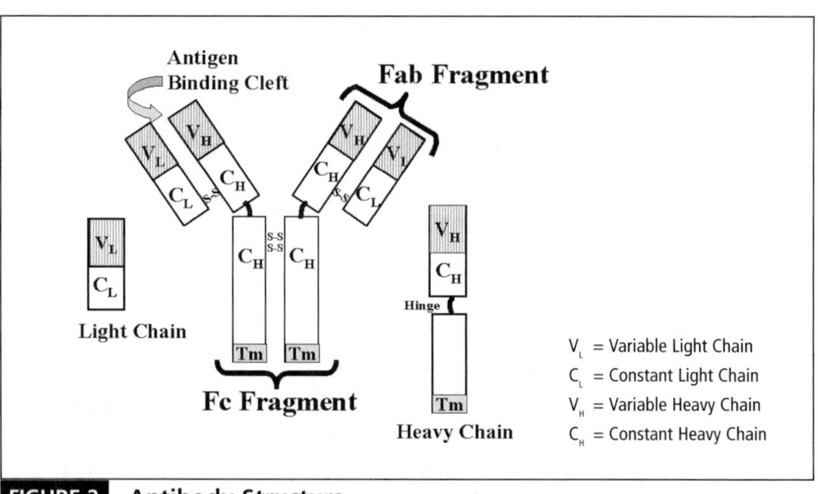

FIGURE 2 Antibody Structure

*Antibodies are tetrameric polypeptides (dimers of dimers), comprising two identical copies of a light chain and a heavy chain, covalently bound together by disulfide bonds (**S-S**). The combined variable regions of the light and heavy chains (Fab fragment) form antigen binding clefts; note that antibodies are therefore bivalent, possessing two clefts for binding identical antigen. Alternative splicing of mRNA coding for the heavy chain can either include or excise an extra stretch of nucleotides coding for a transmembrane domain (Tm) at the C-terminus of the antibody (see Figure 3). If this transmembrane domain is not excised, the antibody will get stuck in the B cell membrane, while splicing of the transmembrane domain allows secretion of the antibody. The heavy chain possesses a flexible hinge in its mid-region, allowing antibodies to twist and bend in order to achieve optimal binding to their specific antigen.*

b) Constant regions of light chains come in one of two varieties, defining the light chain subtype: kappa (κ) or lambda (λ)

c) **Both heavy chain and light chain variable regions are created by genetic recombination events, allowing generation of up to 10^{12} unique sequences** (see Figure 3)

d) The heavy and light chain variable regions intertwine, forming a cleft to bind to antigen—**therefore specificity of an antibody for its antigen is determined by the sequences of heavy and light chain variable regions**

TABLE 1 Characteristics of IG Subtypes

CHARACTERISTICS OF IG SUBTYPES

Subtype	Characteristics
IgM	• Secreted by newly activated naïve B cells • **Marker of primary exposure to antigen** • **Forms pentamers in serum,** J chain joins the monomers by binding to their constant regions • Fixes complement well
IgD	• Expressed with IgM on the surface of naïve B cells
IgG	• Secreted by differentiated/memory B cells • **Marker of re-exposure to antigen** • Always monomeric in serum • Fixes complement well • **Crosses the placenta**
IgE	• Secreted by differentiated/memory B cells • **Causes allergy/asthma by binding to receptors on mast cells and basophils and inducing degranulation** • **Kills parasites** by inducing eosinophil-mediated ADCC
IgA	• Secreted by **mucosal B cells** • Forms dimers, joined by J chain binding to constant region • Epithelial cells translocate IgA dimers by binding to the J chain, and then exocytose the IgA on the mucosal surface, **resulting in high IgA levels in mucosal secretions**

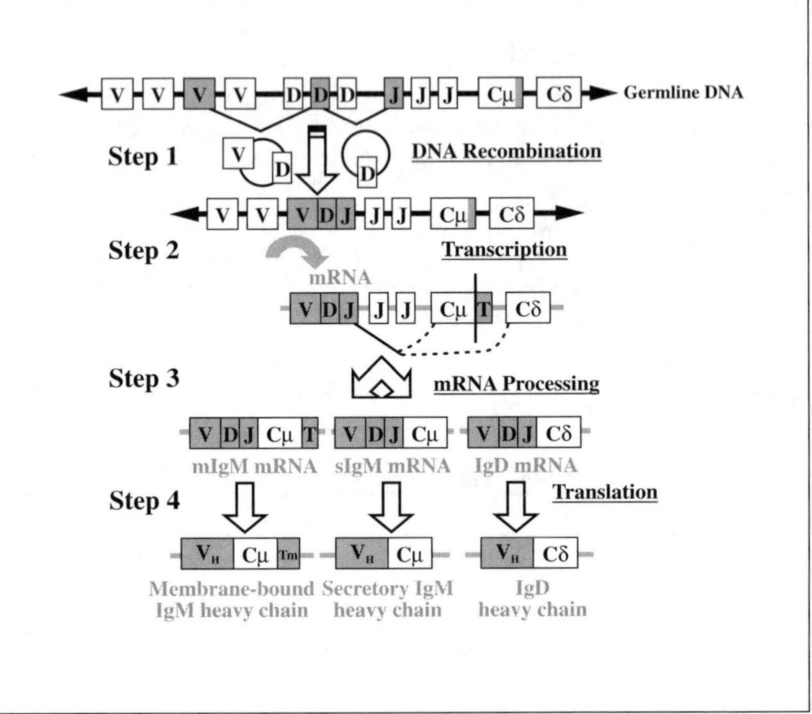

FIGURE 3 Recombination of Antibody Genes

Antibody diversity is generated by recombination of DNA cassettes to create a variable region for both the light and heavy chains of an antibody (only heavy chain recombination is depicted here). The germline DNA of all cells contains hundreds of Variable (V) and dozens of Diversity (D) and Joining (J) segments in the immunoglobulin loci, each of which can be randomly recombined to become part of a gene coding for antibody. Step 1) The first recombination event fuses a randomly selected D region with a J region, excising from the chromosome all the DNA in between. This is followed by recombination joining a random V segment with the D–J fusion product, again excising intervening DNA from the chromosome. Step 2) mRNA is transcribed from the 5′ leader sequence of the V–D–J segment to the 3′ terminus of the genes coding for the IgM (Cμ) and IgD (Cδ) constant regions. Step 3) Nucleotides intervening between the V–D–J variable region and the IgM and IgD constant region genes are excised from the mRNA, resulting in either mature IgM or IgD mRNA. Due to alternative splicing, naïve B cells co-express IgM and IgD bearing the same variable region on the cell surface. In addition, the 3′ end of the IgM constant region gene (Cμ) contains a second alternative splice site followed by a short transmembrane domain (Tm). If the Tm is not spliced out, the IgM will attach to the cell membrane (mIgM) and serve as a surface receptor. Following B cell activation, the Tm will be spliced out, allowing the activated B cell to secrete its antibody (sIgM). IgD is not normally secreted. Step 4) Translation of the mature mRNA into its polypeptide product.

3) The antibody molecule can be divided into domains (see Figure 2)

    a) **The Fab domain is the antigen-binding region** formed by the variable regions of heavy and light chains

    b) **The Fc domain is the constant portion of the heavy chain which defines the antibody subtype (e.g., IgM vs. IgG)**

4) **By alternative splicing of mRNA** transcribed from the recombined antibody gene, **the B cell can either express a membrane bound form of the antibody** (the B cell receptor) or can remove the membrane binding section of the constant region allowing **secretion of the antibody** (see Figures 2 and 3)

5) Allelic exclusion

    a) **Allelic exclusion ensures all the antibody expressed by a given B cell is specific for the same antigen (to a first approximation)**

    b) After recombination successfully generates a functional heavy chain gene, a signal is sent to the cell to stop recombining the other allele, thereby excluding expression of both alleles

    c) Allelic exclusion also functions during recombination of the light chain allele

    d) Therefore all antibodies express only one heavy chain allele and one light chain allele, and thus can make antibodies with only one variable region specificity (to a first approximation)

b. B cells develop in the bone marrow, then migrate to lymphatic tissues to seek out the antigen for which they are specific

c. Antigen

1) Antigen is broadly defined as any molecule to which an immune response can be generated

2) Practically speaking, most antigens are proteins; however, antibodies can be generated to any chemical, including those not normally found in the body

d. **Clonal Selection Activation** (see Figure 4)

1) The body contains billions of B cells, each of which produces antibody with a unique antigen-binding specificity

2) Appropriate antibody responses are generated when antigen binds to, or selects, the few clones of B cells among the billions in the body whose antibody is specific for that antigen

3) The antigen-specific B cells are then activated (see the following) and given signals to proliferate, resulting in selective expansion of only those clones reactive to the antigen

e. Two-Signal Lymphocyte Activation

1) Antigen cross-links antibody in the B cell membrane, resulting in Signal 1, the first of two signals required to activate the B cell

2) **Despite antigen ligation of surface antibody, B cells cannot be fully activated to make antibody against protein antigens unless T-helper cells are available to provide a second stimulatory signal (Signal 2)**

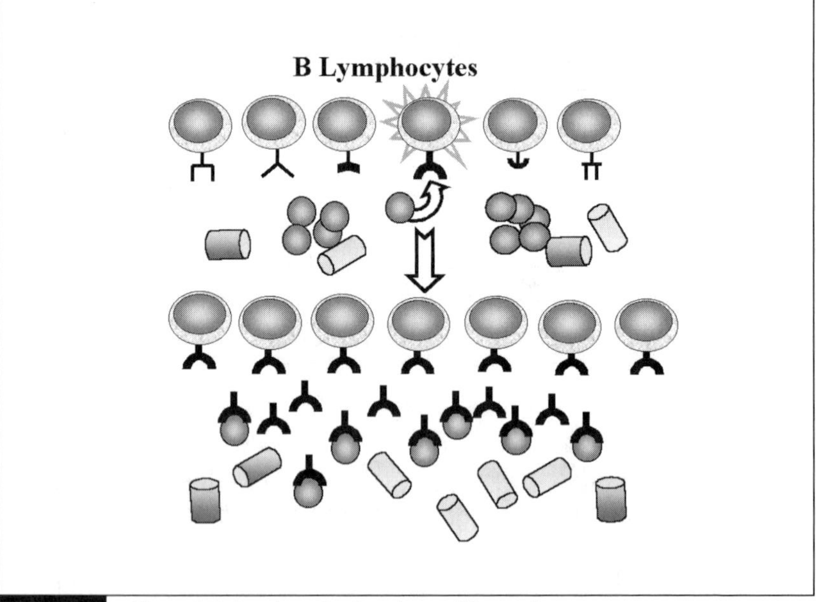

FIGURE 4 **Clonal Selection Activation of Lymphocytes**

Naïve B cells with diverse antigen-specific receptors circulate through the lymphatics scanning for an activating antigen. Antigens selectively activate B cells whose antibody receptors specifically recognize the antigen. This leads to proliferation and expansion of those particular B cell clones, which then secrete an excess of antibody to clear the antigen from the host.

3) Signal 2

   a) T cell second signal is provided by surface binding of CD40-ligand on the T cell to CD40 on the B cell, as well as by T cell secretion of helper cytokines such as IL-4, IL-10, and IL-13, which enable B cell proliferation and activation of antibody secretion

   b) The second signal provided by T cells is a safety check to prevent B cells from being activated by host antigens

   c) If a B cell binds to antigen but no T cell has been activated by that same antigen, the B cell undergoes apoptosis

4) **There are two classes of T-cell independent antigens which can stimulate B cell production of antibody without T cell help (e.g., without Signal 2)**

   a) Type 1 T-cell independent antigens

      i) These are all mitogens, which inherently stimulate B cell proliferation without binding to the B-cell receptor (e.g., without generating Signal 1)

      ii) The most famous Type 1 T-cell independent antigen is gram negative bacterial lipopolysaccharide (endotoxin), which binds to CD14 and the Toll-4 receptor on the B cell surface

      iii) **Thus lipopolysaccharide, like all Type 1 T-cell independent antigens, bypasses both Signal 1 and Signal 2** and generates a completely different activating signal (lipopolysaccharide binding to CD14 and Toll-4)

   b) Type 2 T-cell independent antigens

      i) Large polysaccharide molecules with multiple repeating sequences, such as those found in bacterial cell walls, can cross-link B cell receptors so effectively that T cell help is not needed for activation

      ii) **Thus, unlike Type I T-cell independent antigen, Type II T-cell independent antigens do bind to the B cell receptor to generate Signal 1, and bypass Signal 2 by generating such a powerful Signal 1 that Signal 2 is simply irrelevant**

BOLDERO LIB UCM

f. B cells activated in the presence of T-helper cells differentiate into plasma cells that can produce antibodies—**these are the primary effectors of humoral immunity**

g. **Differentiation into plasma cells occurs in the germinal centers of lymph nodes**

h. During plasma cell differentiation, two processes occur that change the nature of the secreted antibodies

   1) **Class switching**

      a) Deletion of intervening DNA allows an antibody to switch from IgM to IgG subtype (see Figure 5)

      b) Additional class switching allows change from IgG to IgE to IgA

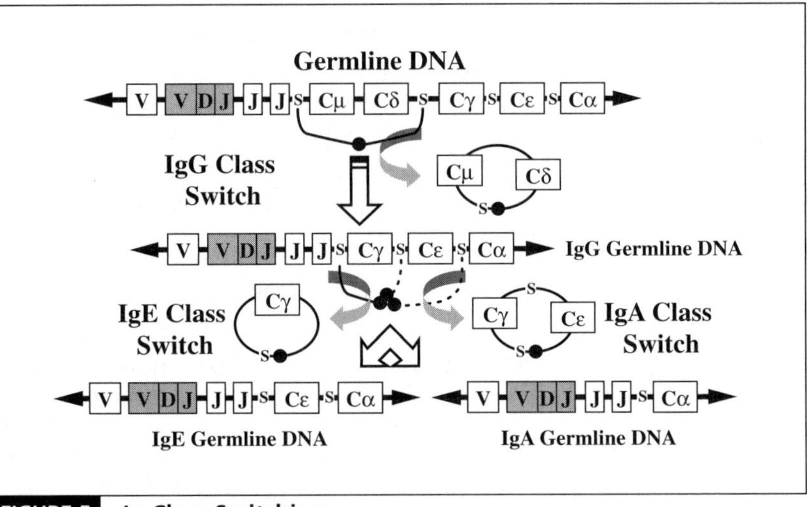

FIGURE 5 **Ig Class Switching**

Class switching is the swap of the same variable region onto a different heavy chain constant region, e.g., switching an IgM to an IgG during an immune response. B cells undergo this process in the germinal centers of lymph nodes. Class switching occurs via intrachromosomal recombination targeted to special switch sites (S) 5′ to each constant region gene. All IgMs must class-switch to IgG before proceeding to IgE or IgA. During this initial class switch, DNA coding for the constant region of IgM and IgD (Cμ and Cδ) are excised from the chromosome. Subsequent class switching from IgG can either proceed to IgE or to IgA without passing through IgE first. Note that IgM and IgD are the only two classes that can be concurrently expressed. In addition, since class-switching involves deletion of intervening DNA, it cannot be reversed (thus IgG cannot class-switch back to IgM).

c) IgM is thus a marker for naïve and newly activated B cells, whereas IgG is a marker of a mature plasma cell or a memory B cell

d) **Class switching cannot occur without T cell help** (thus T-cell independent antigens can only stimulate IgM antibodies, not IgG)

2) **Affinity maturation**

a) During the differentiation of B cells to plasma cells, the germline DNA coding for the antibody is susceptible to a million-fold increase in its mutation rate

b) As the maturing plasma cells continue to divide, this increased mutation rate generates individual clones with slightly different germ-line DNA, coding for antibodies of slightly different specificity

c) Continued binding to antigen is necessary to maintain the survival of plasma cells, and those plasma cells whose mutations confer a higher affinity binding to the stimulating antigen are selected to survive and continue replicating

d) Clones containing mutations that do not improve the antibody affinity for the antigen are unable to compete for continued antigen binding and die

e) Affinity maturation occurs concurrently with class switching

f) **The result is that IgG antibodies are always of significantly higher affinity for the stimulating antigen than were their IgM precursors**

i. Plasma cells migrate to the bone marrow or mucosa when affinity maturation is complete, and there secrete antibodies into the systemic circulation

j. During generation of plasma cells, memory cells with identical antibody specificities are also formed, which can persist for decades in the host

2. $\alpha\beta$ T Lymphocytes

a. $\alpha\beta$ refers to the T-cell receptor, which is a dimer of α chains and β chains (see Figure 6)

1) Like antibodies, the variable region of T-cell receptors are generated via recombination of multiple variable DNA segments

2) Like antibodies, T-cell receptors are regulated by allelic exclusion, so all the T-cell receptors expressed by a given T cell possess identical specificity

3) **Unlike antibodies, T-cell receptors do not directly bind to stimulating antigen—instead antigen must be "presented" to the T cell in the context of Major Histocompatibility Molecules** (see Figures 6 and 7)

b. T cells derive from the bone marrow, but early precursor cells leave the bone marrow and migrate to the thymus for education

1) In the thymus, autoantigen is presented to maturing T cells in the context of MHC molecules

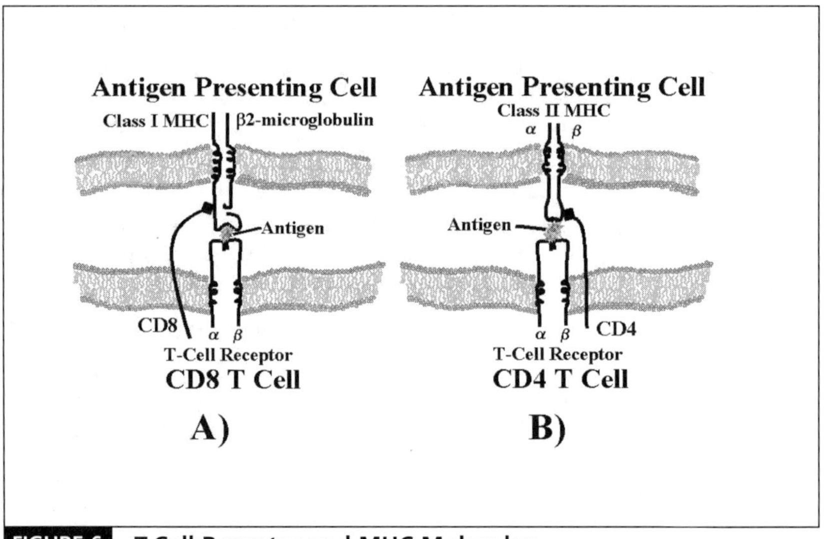

FIGURE 6 T-Cell Receptor and MHC Molecules

The αβ T-cell receptor (TCR) is a heterodimer of α and β chains. The α and β chains have variable N-termini, akin to antibodies, which form the contact area to bind with antigen/MHC complexes. Like antibodies, the diversity of the α and β variable regions is generated via intrachromosomal recombination. A) Class I MHC molecules are heterodimers of Class I MHC α chains and β-2 microglobulin, a chaperone protein that stabilizes Class I MHC molecules at the cell surface. B) Class II MHC molecules are heterodimers comprising α and β MHC chains. Both the α and β chains of Class II molecules bind to antigen, however only the Class I MHC α chain binds to antigen (i.e., β-2 microglobulin does not bind to antigen). The CD8 molecule expressed on cytotoxic T lymphocytes binds to a conserved element on the α chain of Class I MHC, whereas CD4 binds to a conserved element on the β chain of Class II MHC.

2) Those T cells that bind too avidly to the MHC/autoantigen complexes are deemed autoreactive and are induced to undergo apoptosis **(negative selection)**

3) Those T cells that cannot bind at all to the MHC/autoantigen complexes do not receive a survival signal and undergo apoptosis, while those that bind loosely do receive a survival signal **(positive selection)**

4) **Result is a T-cell population which has two crucial characteristics**

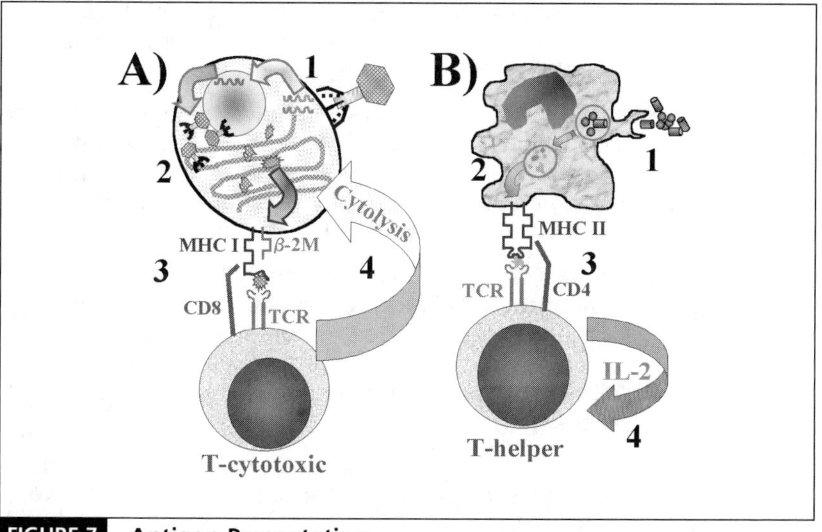

FIGURE 7 **Antigen Presentation**

Antigen presentation to T-cytotoxic (CD8+) and T-helper cells (CD4+). A) 1. A host cell is infected by an intracellular pathogen (virus in this example). 2. As progeny virions are produced, viral antigens are pumped into the endoplasmic reticulum where they bind to Class I Major Histocompatibility Complex (MHC I) proteins. 3. Covalent interaction with the chaperone protein, β-2 microglobulin, allows surface expression of the MHC I polypeptide, which presents viral antigen bound to a groove at its tip. The CD8 protein on the T-cytotoxic cell binds to the MHC I molecule, stabilizing the interaction between the T-cell receptor (TCR) and the MHC I-antigen complex. 4. The result is activation of the T-cytotoxic cell, which then lyses the host cell to expose the intracellular virus. B) 1. A phagocyte ingests extracellular microbes and degrades them in the phagolysosome. 2. Degraded microbial fragments are loaded onto Class II MHC molecules in the phagolysosome and the MHC II-antigen complexes are transported to the cell surface. 3. CD4 binds to MHC II, stabilizing the interaction between the TCR and the MHC II-antigen complex. 4. The result is activation of the T-helper cell, which autocrine stimulates its own proliferation by secreting IL-2.

a) T cells only respond to antigen presented in the context of MHC molecules (due to positive selection)

b) T cells do not respond to most self-antigens, even if in the context of MHC molecules (due to negative selection)

c. Also in the thymus, αβ T cells differentiate to become CD4+ or CD8+

1) T-cell precursors entering the thymus are double negative (CD4-CD8-)

2) Prior to selection, they begin to express both CD8 and CD4, which respectively preferentially bind to Class I and Class II MHC

3) CD8 ligation of Class I MHC and CD4 ligation of Class II MHC add a certain affinity to the interaction between the T-cell receptor and MHC, which may result in too strong an affinity (negative selection) or just the right affinity (positive selection)

4) Those T cells positively selected by the combined ligation of the T-cell receptor and CD8 with Class I MHC are induced to shut down expression of CD4, while those positively selected by the T-cell receptor and CD4 binding to Class II MHC are induced to shut down CD8 expression

5) The result is a population of CD4-CD8+ T cells restricted to Class I MHC, and CD4+CD8- T cells restricted to Class II MHC

d. αβ CD4+ T cells

1) **These are the classic T-helper cells that regulate immune responses**

2) After initial activation, they may differentiate into Th1 or Th2 cells (see Figure 8)

3) Th1 cells

a. Act against small, **phagocytosable, intracellular** pathogens

b. Characterized by secretion of Interleukin (IL)-2, **Interferon (IFN)**-γ, and Lymphotoxin (LT)-α

c. Induce potent cell-mediated, inflammatory responses

d. Antibody stimulation is less marked

e. Uninhibited Th1 cells are implicated in autoimmunity (e.g., Multiple Sclerosis)

4) Th2 cells

a. Act against large, **non-phagocytosable, extracellular** helminths

b. Characterized by secretion of **IL-4**, IL-5, IL-10, and IL-13

c. Markedly induce antibody production, also induce class switching to IgE

d. Act to suppress Th1-mediated inflammatory responses, thereby shifting immune activity from cell-mediated to humoral immunity

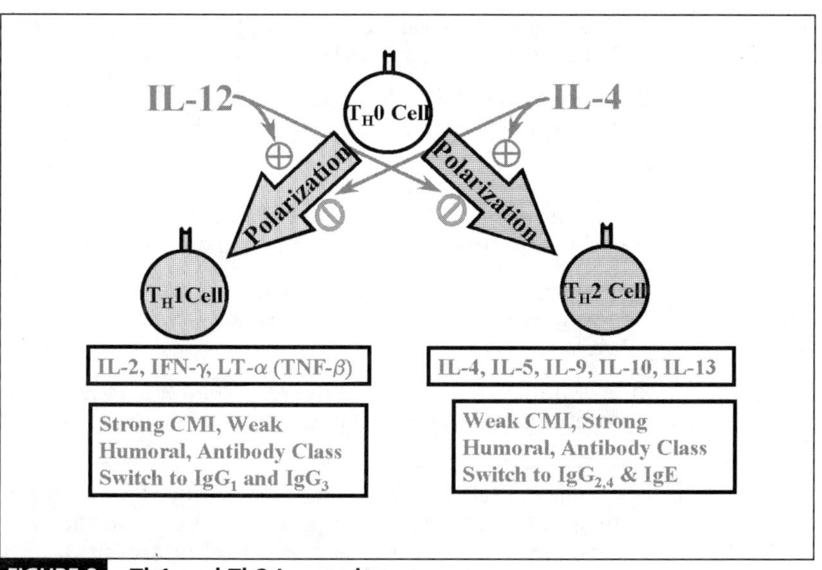

FIGURE 8 Th1 and Th2 Immunity

Summary of Th1/Th2 induction. IL-12 polarizes the naïve Th0 cell to differentiate along the Th1 pathway, and inhibits differentiation to the Th2 phenotype, while IL-4 acts reciprocally. Th1 cells induce strong cell-mediated immune (CMI) responses and weaker antibody responses, while Th2 cells suppress CMI and generate strong humoral responses. Th1 cells induce B cell class switching to IgG_1 and IgG_3, which fix complement and bind to Fcγ receptors on phagocytes. Th2 cells induce B cell class switching to IgG_4, which does not fix complement, does not bind to Fcγ receptors on phagocytes, but does cross the placenta. Th2 cells also induce class switching to IgE. As a result, Th1 immunity is protective against phagocytosable pathogens, whereas Th2 immunity is protective against large, non-phagocytosable eukaryotes, such as helminths.

BORDERO LIBR

e. Uninhibited Th2 cells implicated in allergic/atopic disorders and asthma

f. A shift from dominance of Th1 to Th2 cells correlates with progression of AIDS

5) Th3 cells

a) More recently described, serve as major regulators of mucosal immunity

b) Characterized by high levels of transforming growth factor (TGF)-β production

c) Induce IgA secretion by B cells

d) Responsible for Oral Tolerance (see III.B. Tolerance, 5)

e. αβ CD8+ T cells

1) **These are cytotoxic T cells (CTLs) that act against viruses and cancers by lysing host cells** (see Figure 7)

2) CTLs expose intracellular pathogens to the immune system by destroying host cells harboring the pathogens

3. γδ T cells

a. Express a special T-cell receptor called the γδ receptor, coded for by entirely separate genes than αβ receptor

1) γδ receptor is less polymorphic than αβ receptor, but is also generated by recombination of variable gene segments

2) Like antibody and unlike the αβ T-cell receptor, γδ T-cell receptors can directly bind to certain antigens to become activated

b. Act against evolutionarily conserved antigens in common commensal bacteria and fungi, as well as autoantigens released by necrosed cells (e.g., heat shock proteins)

c. Activated γδ T cells possess cytotoxic activity akin to CD8 cells, and also secrete a broad range of pro-inflammatory molecules to stimulate the rest of the immune response

d. They are thus presumed to be an evolutionarily primitive (homologues seen in boneless fish) early response element to danger

4. Natural Killer (NK) Lymphocytes

a. Do NOT express T-cell receptor or B-cell receptor

b. **Express inhibitory receptors that bind to Class I MHC mol-**

ecules, so NK cells are inhibited from killing host cells that express Class I MHC

c. Certain viruses escape CD8+ T cell-mediated destruction by down-regulating Class I MHC expression by their host cell, but the host cell then becomes susceptible to destruction by NK cells

d. Certain cancers similarly attempt CD8+ T-cell escape and may fall prey to NK cells

II. MAJOR HISTOCOMPATIBILITY COMPLEX (MHC)

A. General Characteristics

1. **The MHC is responsible for immune recognition of self vs. nonself**, thus organ donation requires matching some or all of the MHC genes from an organ donor with the MHC genes of the recipient—this is the so-called organ "match"
2. MHC genes code for proteins expressed on the surfaces of cells
3. **In humans, MHC proteins are called Human Leukocyte Antigens (HLA)—that is, HLA is synonymous with human MHC**
4. There are six different HLA genes, 3 Class I MHC genes and 3 Class II MHC genes
    a. Human Class I MHC genes are known as HLA-A, HLA-B, and HLA-C
    b. Human Class II MHC genes are known as HLA-DP, HLA-DQ, and HLA-DR
5. **MHC Class I and II are the most polymorphic genes known in humans**, meaning no other genes have been found which have so many different alleles in the population
6. MHC genes are codominant, meaning that each individual expresses one allele of the gene inherited from the mother and one allele of the gene inherited from the father, so each person expresses two alleles of each of the HLA-A, HLA-B, HLA-C, and HLA–DP, HLA-DQ, HLA-DR
7. MHC Class I is expressed by almost every cell in the body, with red blood cells and sperm cells notable exceptions
8. MHC Class II is constitutively expressed only by professional antigen presenting cells

   a. Macrophages, B lymphocytes, and dendritic cells are professional antigen presenting cells
   b. Endothelial cells can be induced to express Class II MHC by exposure to IFN-γ
9. Certain alleles are linked to disease states
   a. HLA-DR4 (the fourth allele of the Class II MHC gene, HLA-DR) is classically associated with inflammatory arthritic disorders
   b. HLA-B27 (the 27th allele of the Class I gene, HLA-B) is associated with Ankylosing Spondylitis

B. Class I MHC (see Figure 7)

1. Utilized to present antigen to CD8+ cytotoxic T cells (CD8 binds to Class I molecule)
2. Transporter of Activating Peptide (TAP) is a pump embedded in the endoplasmic reticulum of all cells, which scavenges the cytoplasm for loose proteins
3. TAP pumps proteins into the proteasome, a garbage disposal unit which chops up the incoming proteins and then loads the peptide fragments onto Class I MHC molecules
4. Class I MHC molecules loaded with peptides in the endoplasmic reticulum are then transported to the cell surface, where they present the antigen to any T cell passing by
5. **Therefore Class I MHC presents intracellular, cytoplasmic peptides formed from normal cellular metabolism or the metabolism of intracellular pathogens (e.g., viruses, *Chlamydia*, etc.)**

C. Class II MHC (see Figure 7)

1. Utilized to present antigen to CD4+ T-helper cells (CD4 binds to Class II molecule)
2. Phagocytic cells degrade ingested particles in the phagolysosome
3. Class II MHC molecules are then transported into the phagolysosome and digested peptides are loaded onto the Class II MHC molecules
4. The peptide-loaded Class II MHC molecules are then transported to the cell surface

5. **Class II MHC presents extracellular antigens, having entered the cell via the phagolysosomal pathway**

D. Transplant Immunology

1. The MHC Match
   a. MHC types of organ donors and organ recipients are checked against one another to find close matches
   b. Each child gets one set of HLA alleles from both parents
   c. HLA genes are co-dominant, so alleles inherited from both parents are expressed in the child
   d. Since both parents also have two sets of alleles (total of four sets between the two parents), and each child gets one set from mom and one set from dad (the child gets two of the four parental alleles), siblings have a 25% chance of inheriting identical HLA alleles from their parents (1/2 chance of getting same maternal alleles × 1/2 chance of getting same paternal alleles = 1/4 chance of getting same both alleles)
   e. On the other hand, since children express both paternal and maternal alleles, they will typically not be matched to either of their parents, unless mom and dad both have identical HLA alleles (a situation only seen with extreme in-breeding)
   f. Thus sibling organ donors are the best chance for a perfect HLA match
   g. Because of immunosuppressive drugs, perfect matches are not required for successful organ donation, but the more HLA alleles are matched, the better grafts do on average
2. Hyperacute Graft Rejection
   a. Occurs within minutes of transplant
   b. Seen in MHC mismatched recipient who has been previously sensitized to the donor's MHC type (by pregnancy, blood transfusions, prior graft, etc)
   c. Caused by preformed antibodies circulating in recipient's serum
   d. Cannot be reversed, requires removal of graft
3. Acute Graft Rejection
   a. Occurs within weeks of transplant

b. Seen in MHC mismatched recipient not previously exposed to the donor's MHC type

c. Caused by CD8+ cytotoxic T cells reacting to foreign MHC molecules

d. Typically reversible with immunosuppressive agents such as cyclosporin or FK-506, both of which inhibit calcineurin-induced activation of IL-2 secretion from T cells, thereby inhibiting T cell activation

4. Chronic Graft Rejection

a. Occurs over months to years after transplant

b. Caused by antibody damage to vascular system, based upon MHC mismatch

c. Cannot be reversed with immunosuppressives

III. BASIC CONCEPTS

A. Innate vs. Specific Immunity

1. Innate Immunity

a. Skin

1) Serves as a structural barrier against microbial entry into the host

2) Also colonized by commensal organisms which compete for nutrients thereby inhibiting growth of pathogens

b. Mucous membranes

1) **Bathed in fluids containing lysozyme**, an enzyme which lyses bacterial cell walls

2) **Mucosal fluids also contain high concentration of secretory IgA**, which blocks microbial adhesion to mucosal epithelium

3) Covered with cilia that sweep away particulates and microbes

c. Chemical barriers

1) The body uses toxic pH levels in the stomach to protect the GI tract, and pH levels in the dermis and vagina inhibit overgrowth of bacteria

2) **Chelation of iron during inflammation is a very potent inhibitor of microbial growth**, explaining why iron-binding proteins such as transferrin and ferritin go up during inflammation (so-called acute phase reactants)

d. Phagocytes (from the Greek "phago" = eat, "cyte" = cell, "phagocyte" = eater cell)

1) Neutrophils, monocyte/macrophages, eosinophils, and dendritic cells are professional phagocytes

2) Phagocytes migrate through the peripheral vasculature and are recruited into tissue at the start of an inflammatory response

a) **Recruitment begins with local elicitation of chemotactic cytokines, called chemokines, secreted by injured cells** or by stressed cells neighboring the injured cells

b) Chemokines diffuse into the bloodstream, setting up a concentration gradient allowing phagocytes to home-in on the source

c) Chemokines, as well as bacterial antigens such as endotoxin, also activate the phagocytes, causing them to express adhesion molecules on their surface

3) When phagocytes reach the source of the chemokine gradient, they undergo a **three-step process known as extravasation**, allowing them to leave the vasculature and enter peripheral tissue (see Figure 9)

a) **Step 1**: binding to **selectin** molecules on the endothelial cells causes the phagocyte to roll along the inner wall of the blood vessel

b) **Step 2**: binding to **ICAM** causes the phagocyte to stop rolling and firmly **adhere** to the endothelium

c) **Step 3**: the phagocyte undergoes **diapedesis**, squeezing in between the endothelial cells and binding to PECAM at the endothelial cell junction, allowing it to crawl out of the blood vessel towards the source of the chemokines

4) Phagocytosis is triggered by binding of one of several receptors on the phagocyte to its target ligand

a) **The phagocyte Fcγ receptor binds to the constant regions (Fc) of IgG antibodies (γ = IgG, thus Fcγ = receptor for the Fc of IgG)** allowing ingestion of any particle attached to the antibody variable region

b) The phagocyte Complement Receptor 3 (CR3) binds to complement fragments deposited on microbes

c) **Phagocyte Toll-family receptors bind directly to conserved elements in microbial cell walls,** such as gram negative lipopolysaccharide (endotoxin)

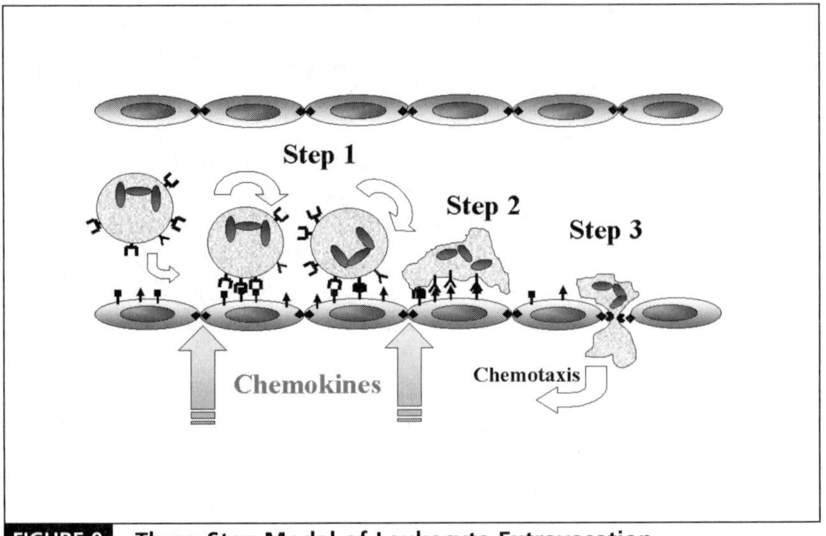

FIGURE 9 Three-Step Model of Leukocyte Extravasation

Leukocyte extravasation from the intravascular compartment into parenchyma is a three-step process. Step 1) Inflammatory cytokines released at the site of infection induce endothelial cells to express selectin molecules on their cell surface (⯒). Chemokines diffuse from the site of infection into the blood stream, creating a concentration gradient to attract leukocytes from the intravascular compartment. Such chemokines also induce leukocytes to express selectin-ligands on their cell surface (Ɏ). Leukocytes following the chemokine gradient migrate towards the endothelium neighboring the site of infection and the low affinity interaction between selectins and selectin-ligands results in rolling of the leukocyte along the endothelium. Step 2) Binding of selectins to selectin-ligands induces higher affinity adhesins, such as ICAM (Y) on endothelial cells and LFA (↑) on leukocytes, to be expressed. These higher affinity interactions cause the leukocytes to cease rolling and firmly adhere to the endothelium. Step 3) Freed from the shear forces of blood flow, the leukocytes crawl across the endothelium and diapedese between the endothelial cells, disrupting the binding of PECAM-PECAM homodimers which hold neighboring endothelial cells together (◆◆). The leukocytes unzip the PECAM homodimers and use the PECAM molecules on either side as traction to propel the leukocytes out of the blood vessel and into tissue. Subsequently the leukocytes crawl through the tissue along the chemokine concentration gradient, leading back to the site of infection.

5) Following phagocytosis, the phagosome fuses with lysosomes and neutrophil or eosinophil granules, the contents of which mediate killing of any microbes in the phagolysosome
6) Phagocytosis also stimulates the leukocyte to undergo the **respiratory or oxidative burst**
    a) NADPH oxidase assembles on the phagosome membrane, generating superoxide anion (O_2–) from oxygen
    b) Superoxide is converted to one of a variety of toxic metabolites
        i) Superoxide dismutase converts the superoxide to hydrogen peroxide (H_2O_2), which has intrinsic antimicrobial properties
        ii) **In neutrophils, myeloperoxidase combines peroxide with chloride anions to generate hypochlorite** ($HClO^-$, common house bleach) which is highly toxic to microbes in the phagosome
7) **Importance of phagocytes demonstrated by the markedly elevated risk of death from infection in neutropenic patients**

e. Fever
1) **Fever is a host response to infection**
2) **Systemic IL-1, IL-6, or TNF, generated in response to bacterial pyrogens such as lipopolysaccharide, cause the hypothalamic thermostat to reset higher**
3) Growth of some microbes is optimized to normal body temperature, and fever results in a partial inhibition of their growth
4) Phagocytosis and the respiratory burst are more efficient at higher temperatures

f. Complement (see Figure 10)
1) A reactive cascade of serum proteins resulting in three beneficial effects
    a) The generation of protein fragments chemotactic for leukocytes, (e.g. C3a and C5a)
    b) **Opsonization** (from the Greek for "to make palatable"), or the coating of microbes with host protein fragments (e.g., C3b) that enable phagocytosis

c) Generation of the **membrane attack complex** (MAC, comprised of C5 to C8), which punches holes in microbial cell membranes

2) The complement components C1 to C4 have **serine protease activity**, activating the next component in the cascade by cleaving the next component in two, thereby exposing the active enzyme site of that next component

3) At each step along the cascade, enzymatic serine protease activity results in significant amplification of the response, meaning that activation of one molecule of a complement component leads to activation of hundreds or thousands of the next molecule in the cascade

4) **There are two pathways to activate the complement cascade**

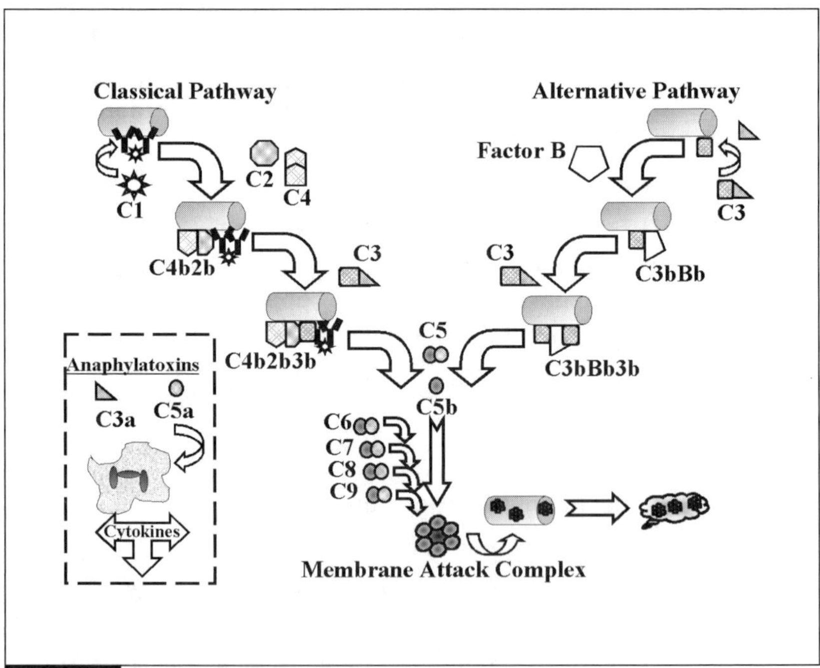

FIGURE 10 **The Complement Cascade**

The complement cascade can be initiated by binding of C1 to the Fc domains of antibody (the Classical Pathway), or by direct binding of C3 to microbial glycolipids (the Alternative Pathway). See text for a description of each component in the cascade.

a) The Classical Pathway

i) **The constant region of antibodies**, or acute phase reactants such as C-reactive protein, bind to C1, bringing it in close proximity to a microbe

ii) C1 acts as a serine protease to cleave C2 and C4, forming C4b2b

iii) C4b2b is known as C3 convertase, because it cleaves thousands of copies of C3 into C3a and C3b

iv) C3a is known as an anaphylatoxin because it binds to mast cells and basophils and stimulates massive release of histamine, generating local inflammation

v) C3b deposited onto microbes opsonizes them, allowing binding of phagocytes via the CR3 receptor

vi) C3b also joins C4b2b to form C4b2b3b, which converts C5 to C5a and C5b

vii) Like C3a, C5a is also an anaphylatoxin, while C5b initiates the membrane attack complex formation by successive binding of C6, C7, C8, and C9

viii) The membrane attack complex punches a donut-shaped hole in the microbial cell membrane, resulting in osmotic lysis

b) The Alternative Pathway

i) **C3 can directly bind to evolutionarily conserved microbial surface antigens**

ii) This results in spontaneous degradation of C3 to C3a and C3b

iii) Factor B binds to C3b and is then cleaved by Factor D, forming C3bBb

iv) C3bBb is analogous to C4b2b3b of the Classical Pathway, acting as a C5 convertase

v) **Thus, the Alternative and Classical Pathways are initiated by different mechanisms, but have in common every step from C5 convertase forward**

g. Cytokines also have innate immune functions, particularly IL-1 and interferons (see cytokines section)

2. Specific Immunity
   a. **Specificity is provided to immune responses ONLY via B and T lymphocytes**
   b. Specificity of lymphocytes is dependent upon their antigen receptors, which are created during cellular ontogeny by gene recombination events
   c. Unlike innate immunity, specific immunity has memory: the specific immune system respond differently the second time it sees the same antigen/microbe
   d. **Memory**
      1) Memory lymphocytes differentiate following the initial, primary immune response mediated by a particular lymphocyte
      2) Memory cells are long-lived, and continue to re-circulate throughout the body until they again encounter the same antigen that initiated the primary response
      3) **Memory cells are responsible for two important clinical effects**
         a) Vaccination is possible by stimulation of high levels of memory cells
         b) Infections like chicken pox rarely occur twice in the same person due to memory cells induced following the first infection
   e. Primary versus Secondary Immunity
      1) A primary immune response results the first time lymphocytes are activated against a given antigen
      2) Secondary immune responses occur following reactivation of memory cells generated during the primary response
      3) Secondary immunity is faster, more powerful and more specific

B. Tolerance

1. **Tolerance is the lack of immune responses against self-tissues (lack of autoimmunity)**
2. **Since only lymphocytes are specific effectors, tolerance is dependent upon lymphocytic functions**

3. Two general mechanisms of tolerance are Central and Peripheral
   a. Central Tolerance
      1) **Provided by T-cell education during development in the thymus**
      2) As described above, immature T cells which are strongly reactive to self-tissues, undergo negative selection and are induced to apoptose in the thymus
      3) **Central tolerance is imperfect because it is impossible to expose the lymphocytes in the thymus to every possible antigen contained within the human body**
   b. Peripheral Tolerance
      1) **Acts as a crucial backup to central tolerance**
      2) Three major mechanisms of peripheral tolerance
         a) **Antigenic ignorance**
            i) If T cells never see certain self-antigens (called cryptic antigens), they can never respond to them even if they are capable of doing so
            ii) Significant portions of parenchymal organs are never exposed to the immune system unless they are damaged by trauma or inflammation
            iii) Arthritis and diabetes may be examples of diseases where trauma or infection damages tissue, exposing T cells to cryptic antigens against which they have not been centrally tolerized, initiating autoimmunity
         b) **Co-stimulation** (Two-Signal Lymphocyte Activation)
            i) **Like B cells, all $\alpha\beta$ T cells (CD4+ and CD8+) require two signals for activation**
            ii) Professional phagocytes act as antigen presenting cells, complexing ingested antigen with MHC molecules to present to T cells (Signal 1)
            iii) However, professional phagocytes also must provide a second signal to enable T cell activation
            iv) The second signal can be provided by co-stimulatory ligand binding, the most famous of which is B7 on the antigen-presenting cell binding to CD28 on the T cell

v) **In general, phagocytes only provide the second signal for stimulation when the phagocyte recognizes danger in the environment**

a)) Danger is recognized by phagocytes when they are exposed to evolutionarily conserved microbial fragments, such as gram negative lipopolysaccharide, gram positive cell wall lipotechoic acid, or prokaryotic DNA, each of which can bind to specific receptors on the phagocyte

b)) Danger is also recognized by phagocytes when they are exposed to inflammatory cytokines provided by early response elements of the innate immune system (e.g., neutrophils or damaged parenchymal cells leaking IL-1)

vi) Phagocytes recognizing danger signals undergo activation, and are thus primed to provide a second signal to activate T cells, but phagocytes that have not recognized a danger signal are presumed to be presenting antigens from non-threatening particulates which might in fact be host proteins

vii) Thus the second signal requirement is a fail-safe to prevent activation of potentially auto-reactive T cells

viii) **T-cells receiving Signal 1 (MHC/antigen binding to T cell receptor) without Signal 2 become either anergic (tolerized to the antigen for which they are specific) or they apoptose**

5) Oral Tolerance

a) Induced by Th3 cells due to ↑TGF-β production

b) Can induce tolerance to otherwise immunogenic proteins by feeding them to people

c) TGF-β anergizes otherwise reactive T-cells in the gut mucosa

d) Failure of Oral Tolerance leads to Inflammatory Bowel Disease

C. Autoimmunity

1. Due to aberrant lymphocyte (mostly T cell) responses caused by breakage of tolerance
2. Several mechanisms of autoimmunity are known
   a. Reversal of antigenic ignorance
      1) Occurs when inflammation develops in parenchymal tissues
      2) Tissue destruction exposes T cells to autoantigens that had previously been sequestered (so called "cryptic antigens")
      3) T cells potentially reactive to cryptic antigens are not deleted because such antigens are not expressed in the thymus
      4) Since inflammation is ongoing, phagocytes will be exposed to danger signals in the form of inflammatory cytokines, and can present autoantigens to T cells along with a second signal, causing T cell activation

   b. **Molecular Mimicry**
      1) T cells are activated against microbes which have antigens structurally similar to self-antigens
      2) As the immune system revs up, it becomes confused and attacks both the microbe and the self-tissue
      3) Example: rheumatic fever involves immune response to heart valve proteins similar to antigens found in *Streptococcus*

   c. Aberrant cytokine regulation
      1) Out-of-control Th1 or Th2 responses lead to self-destruction
      2) Causes of the loss of control are unclear in most instances
      3) Examples
         a) Th1: tuberculosis and hepatitis kill people due to inflammatory response, not due to direct effects of the microbe/virus
         b) Th2: allergy, asthma, anaphylaxis

IV. CYTOKINES—A BRIEF GUIDE*

TABLE 2 Cytokines

CYTOKINE	CHARACTERISTICS	FUNCTIONS
IL-1 α/β	**Immediate danger signals,** released when cells are damaged—also induces fever	• Initiate inflammation • Endogenous pyrogen
IL-2	**Required for T cell proliferation**	• T cell proliferation
IL-3	Stem cell growth factor	• Stem cell growth factor
IL-4	Stimulates antibody production, linked to atopy and asthma, made by Th2 cells	• Stimulates antibody secretion • Stimulates IgE class switch
IL-5	Eosinophil growth and activation factor, also implicated in asthma/atopy	• Stimulates eosinophil activity • Stimulates basophil activity
IL-6	Systemic marker of inflammation, stimulates acute phase reactants	• Endogenous pyrogen • Acute phase reactant
IL-7	Growth/survival factor for lymphocytes	• Lymphocyte growth factor
IL-8	Chemotactic for neutrophils	• Neutrophil chemoattractant
IL-9	Growth and survival factor for mast cells	• Mast cell growth factor
IL-10	Inhibits expression of almost all cytokines, suppresses inflammation	• General immunosuppressive
IL-11	Stimulates platelet formation, is also anti-inflammatory and ↑ iron absorption in the gut (may explain why platelets ↑ in chronic inflammation and iron deficiency	• Stimulates platelet production • Suppresses inflammation • ↑ iron absorption in the gut
IL-12	Produced by antigen presenting cells, induces Th1 differentiation	• Induces Th1 differentiation
IL-13	Mimics IL-4 functions	• Stimulates antibody secretion • Stimulates IgE class switch

TABLE 2 ***Continued***

CYTOKINE	CHARACTERISTICS	FUNCTIONS
IL-14	May be a B cell growth factor	• ? B cell growth factor
IL-15	Mimics IL-2 functions	• T cell growth factor
IL-16	Chemotactic for CD4 T cells	• Chemotactic for CD4 T cells
IL-17	Non-specific inflammatory stimulator	• Stimulates inflammation
IL-18	Induces production of IFN-γ	• Induces IFN-γ production
IFN-α	Induces anti-viral state in parenchymal cells by altering surface receptors and turning on cellular RNAses and DNAses to chop up invading RNA and DNA	• Induces antiviral state • Activates phagocytes
IFN-β	Secreted by fibroblasts, role unclear in vivo, ? feedback suppression	• ? feedback suppression from inflammation
IFN-γ	Induces antiviral state, markedly stimulates phagocytic activity and Th1 induction	• Induces antiviral state • Stimulates inflammation
TNF	Non-specific inflammatory mediator, endogenous pyrogen, causes cachexia	• Stimulates inflammation • Causes cachexia (formerly called cachectin)
Lymphotoxin-α	Secreted only by Th1 cells, induces apoptosis in target cells, stimulates inflammation	• Induces apoptosis • Stimulates inflammation
TGF-β	Terminates immune responses, induces antigen-specific anergy in T cells, stimulates IgA secretion, causes fibrosis, responsible for oral tolerance	• Causes class switching to IgA • Regulates mucosal immunity • Causes oral tolerance • Causes fibrosis
G-CSF	Stimulates granulocyte production, utilized clinically for neutropenia (Neupogen®)	• Stimulates granulocyte production
GM-CSF	Stimulates granulocyte and monocyte production	• Stimulates granulocyte and monocyte production

*Cytokines in **boldface** are most likely to appear on board exams.

V. IMMUNE ORGAN SYSTEMS

A. Primary Immune Organs (sites of immune cell progenitors)

1. Bone Marrow
    a. The primary hematopoietic organ in the adult human
    b. Possess stem cells which respond to growth factor signals by differentiating into all of the different types of blood
    c. **Also harbors active antibody-producing B cells (plasma cells)**
2. Thymus (see Figure 11)
    a. Secretes cytokines chemotactic for T lymphocyte precursor cells, which leave the bone marrow and migrate to the thymus
    b. Structurally composed of an outer cortex and inner medulla
    c. Cortex
        1) Newly arrived T cells disembark in the subcapsular zone above the cortex, and then migrate down into the cortex
        2) During their migration through the cortex, immature T cells interact with thymic epithelial cells expressing Class I and Class II MHC molecules
        3) **Positive selection occurs here**—that is, only those immature T cells whose receptors are capable of binding to MHC molecules expressed on the thymic cortical epithelium are given survival signals, while T cells with receptors incapable of binding to MHC molecules undergo apoptosis
        4) The positively selected T cells then migrate deeper into the cortex towards the medulla
    d. Medulla
        1) The medulla is populated by bone-marrow derived macrophages and dendritic cells
        2) As the maturing, positively selected T cells migrate to the medulla, they interact with these macrophages and dendritic cells, which also express Class I and Class II MHC molecules

3) Those positively selected T cells that interact too strongly with the MHC molecules on the macrophages and dendritic cells are given a death signal, forcing them to undergo apoptosis

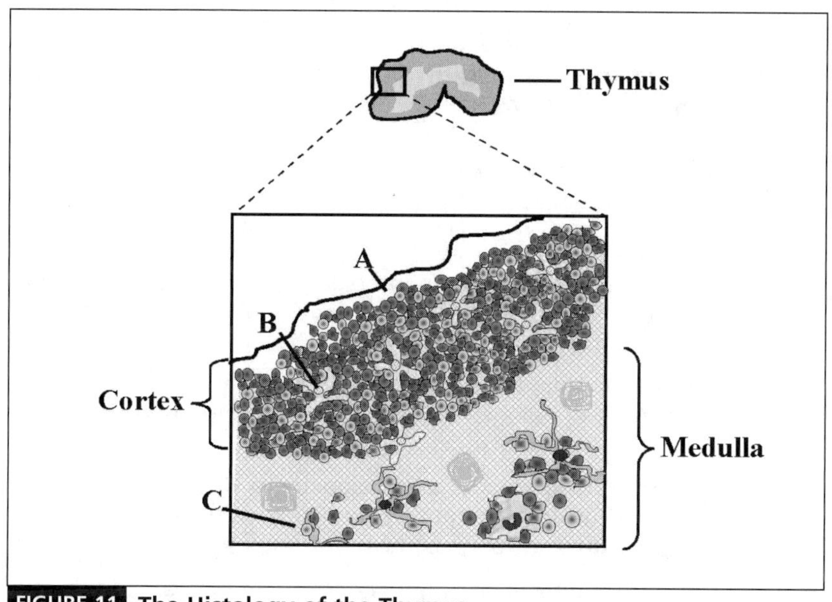

FIGURE 11 The Histology of the Thymus

A magnified perspective reveals three zones within the thymus. A) The subcapsular zone is the entrance point for newly arrived, immature T cells migrating from the vasculature. B) T lymphocytes moving in from the subcapsular zone crowd into the mob of cells in the cortex. The T cells jostle one another for position next to one of the cortical thymic epithelial cells, which present autoantigens in the context of Class I and Class II MHC. More than 90% of T cells will be unable to recognize the complexes of autoantigen and MHC molecules. These cells will be instructed to kill themselves (apoptosis) and will be consumed by local macrophages. Those rare T cells capable of ligating autoantigen plus MHC molecules are given a survival signal, allowing them to migrate further into the thymus (positive selection). C) Upon entering the sparsely populated medulla, the lymphocytes are confronted by interdigitating dendritic cells and macrophages, which again present autoantigen and Class I or Class II MHC molecules. However, dendritic cells and macrophages also express powerful costimulatory molecules. T cells that bind avidly to the autoantigen/MHC complexes on the dendritic cells and macrophages are given a death signal, inducing apoptosis (negative selection). Only those T cells that bind to the cortical epithelial cell autoantigen/MHC complexes (positive selection) but do not bind avidly to the medullary dendritic cell and macrophage autoantigen/MHC complexes (negative selection) survive to exit the thymus and populate the peripheral vasculature and lymphatics.

4) **Thus, negative selection occurs in the thymic medulla,** eliminating potentially autoreactive T cells that survived positive selection in the cortex

5) **99% of T cells entering the thymus undergo apoptosis,** while 1% migrate out of the medulla to enter systemic circulation

B. Secondary Immune organs (sites of initiation of immune responses)

1. Lymph Nodes (See Figure 12)
   a. Aggregations of immune cells placed along lymph channels
   b. Lymph channels drain interstitial fluid from epithelial and parenchymal tissues, routing such fluid back into the vascular compartment via the thoracic duct
   c. In addition, lymph carries antigenic materials floating about in the interstitial fluid to the lymph nodes for sampling by immune cells
   d. **Thus, lymph nodes are designed like filters, allowing the detritus of host and foreign tissues to be accumulated and sifted through by host defense cells**
   e. Like the thymus, lymph nodes can be separated into cortex and medulla
   f. Cortex
      1) The cortex contains multiple follicles, which are masses of B lymphocytes and dendritic cells jammed together
      2) **Follicles without germinal centers are known as primary follicles, while those containing germinal centers are known as secondary follicles**
      3) **Germinal centers are the result of massive B lymphocyte proliferation following activation, and are the locations where class switching and affinity maturation occurs during B cell activation**
      4) T cells occupy the parafollicular areas, which separate the follicles
   g. Medulla
      1) Sparsely populated by migrating lymphocytes and macrophages

2) This is where the vasculature penetrates the node

3) Specialized endothelial cells, called High Endothelial Venules, express adhesion molecules allowing lymphocytes to extravasate across the venules in order to migrate into the lymph node

2. Spleen

   a. Analogous to the lymph nodes filtering lymph of antigen, **the spleen is a giant filter-trap for particulate antigens in the vascular compartment**

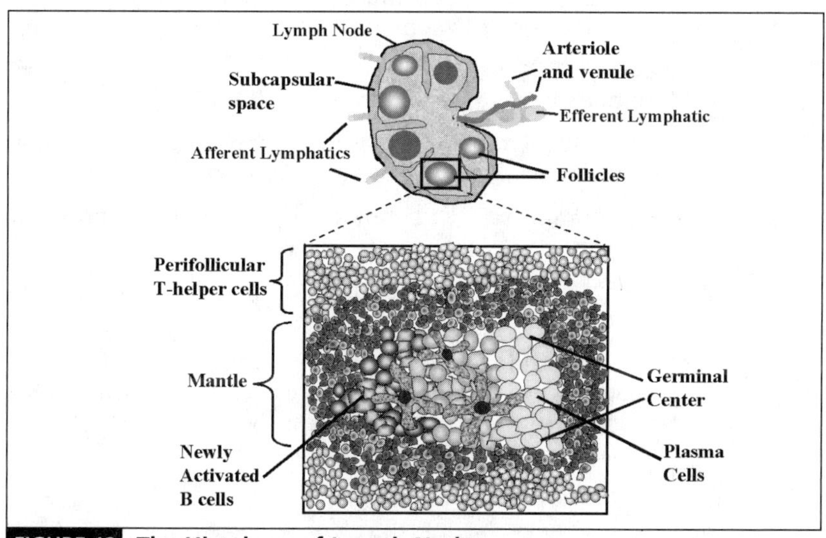

FIGURE 12 The Histology of Lymph Nodes

A lymph node is shown in cross-section, with a magnified image of a secondary follicle. Primary follicles have no germinal center (no central clearing). Secondary follicles have a germinal center, in which large, proliferating B cells are exposed to antigen presented by dendritic cells. Affinity maturation and class switching occur in the germinal centers. In the figure, newly activated B lymphocytes occupy the left-most portion of the germinal center. These cells migrate to the right as they divide, brushing against the follicular dendritic cells, which expose the B cells to antigen in order to further drive affinity maturation and class switching. At the right side of the germinal center are mature effector B cells, called plasma cells, which secrete high-affinity IgG antibodies. From the germinal centers these activated, antibody-secreting cells will migrate into the efferent lymph channel, and from there to bone marrow, submucosa, or spleen to secrete their antibodies into the circulation. A rim of darkly staining B lymphocytes, known as the follicular mantle, surrounds the germinal center. Outside the mantle are CD4+ T-helper cells, occupying the perifollicular areas.

LIBRARY UCM

b. Red pulp

1) Comprises areas dominated by red blood cells and macrophages

2) Arterioles course off the splenic artery, ending in open sinuses surrounded by macrophages

3) Macrophages ingest particulate matter in the blood, and also destroy senescent red cells

c. White pulp

1) Comprised of areas dominated by lymphocytes

2) Arterioles are surrounded by cuffs of lymphocytes (the periarteriolar lymphoid sheaths, or PALS), which form follicles akin to lymph node follicles

3. Mucosal Associated Lymphoid Tissues (MALT)

a. Organized lymphoid tissues found interspersed along the gastrointestinal and respiratory tracts

b. Follicles form in the submucosa, akin to lymph node follicles

c. Th3 cells predominate in MALT, causing B cell class-switching to IgA

d. In the gastrointestinal tract, specialized epithelial cells known as M cells sample the intestinal lumen by endocytosing particulate matter, process the matter and present it as antigen to underlying lymphocytes

VI. HYPERSENSITIVITY REACTIONS

A. Allergic Hypersensitivity (Type 1)

1. IgE-mediated, due to release of vasoactive mediators from mast cells and basophils

a. Following initial exposure to allergen, anti-allergen B cells are induced to class switch to IgE in the presence of IL-4

b. Secreted IgE circulates in the vasculature and binds to receptors on mast cells and basophils which are specific for the constant region of the IgE (Fcε receptors)

c. Upon re-exposure of the allergen, the IgE antibodies sitting on the mast cell and basophil surfaces are cross-linked, causing the cells to degranulate, spilling histamine and leukotrienes into the vasculature

2. Examples = allergies, anaphylaxis, atopic diseases

B. Cytotoxic Hypersensitivity (Type 2)

1. Antibody-mediated, typically IgG binds to antigen on target cell surface, inducing complement lysis, ADCC, or phagocytosis
2. Examples = autoimmune hemolytic anemia, Erythroblastosis Fetalis, pemphigus, Goodpasture's Disease, penicillin-induced anemia, hyperacute transplant rejection

C. Immune Complex Hypersensitivity (Type 3, Arthus Reaction)

1. In the presence of high titer, high affinity IgG antibody, antigens in the serum are bound into large complexes cross-linked by multiple antibodies
2. These large antigen-antibody complexes circulate through the vasculature, and although some are cleared by macrophages in the spleen, some of the complexes deposit in epithelial crevices throughout the body
3. Deposited antigen-antibody complexes bind complement, which attracts neutrophils and induces lytic enzyme release, causing tissue damage
4. Examples = serum sickness, SLE systemic findings, post-infectious glomerulonephritis

D. Delayed Type Hypersensitivity (DTH, Type 4)

1. Induction of Th1 responses causes the local accumulation of phagocytes
2. This response is dependent upon IFN-γ secreted by Th1 cells
3. The result is organized cell-mediated immunity, typified by granulomatous reaction in the subcutaneous or intra-dermal tissues
4. Examples = contact dermatitis, acute/chronic transplant rejection, TB, and poison ivy

VII. IMMUNODEFICIENCIES

A. Primary Immunodeficiencies

TABLE 3 B Lymphocyte Deficiencies

- **Recurrent encapsulated bacterial infections in infants >6 months old**
- **Diagnosis often made by Quantitative Immunoglobulin Analysis (QUIG), revealing abnormal levels of serum immunoglobulin (Ig) subtypes**

DISEASE	PATHOPHYSIOLOGY	PRESENTATION
Bruton's Agammaglobulinemia	• X-linked defect of tyrosine kinase causes defective B cell development	• Always male patients (X-linked) • **No B cells in blood** (normal # of precursors in marrow) • Pts are treated with IVIG
Hyper-IgM Syndrome	• CD40 defect prevents IgG class switching	• QUIG → normal levels of IgM but no IgG • Pts are treated with IVIG
Selective Ig Deficiency	• IgA deficiency most common primary immunodeficiency, affects 1/600 Caucasians (can also have IgG deficiency) • Caused by defects in isotype class switching	• Affected people have **recurrent sinus and respiratory infections, chronic diarrhea, and asthma,** although may be asymptomatic • IgG deficiency causes bronchiectasis • IgA deficient pts (who do have IgG) have anaphylactoid reactions to IgA contained in blood products, **so do not Tx with IVIG** • QUIG → ↓ IgA (or IgG) but normal numbers of peripheral B cells
Common Variable Hypogammaglobulinemia	• An **acquired** defect • Causes ↓ IgG production due to defect in plasma cell differentiation	• Recurrent encapsulated bacterial infections **in patients aged 15–35, with splenomegaly and lymphadenopathy** • QUIG → ↓ antibody levels in the face of normal B cell counts • Treat with monthly IVIG

TABLE 4 T Lymphocyte Deficiencies

- **Recurrent severe viral, fungal, or protozoal infections from infancy**
- **QUIG →normal IgM levels but ↓ IgG and IgA due to defective class switching**

DISEASE	PATHOPHYSIOLOGY	PRESENTATION
DiGeorge's Syndrome	• Embryological defect in pharyngeal pouch 3 and 4 → thymic aplasia which causes T cell deficiency, and parathyroid aplasia	• **Presents with tetany due to hypocalcemia 2° to hypoparathyroidism** • **Syndromic facies** (micrognathia, short philtrum), and congenital cardiac defects • ↓CD4 and CD8 T cells
Ataxia-Telangiectasia	• Autosomal recessive defect in DNA repair • Causes thymic dysfunction • B cells develop normally	• **Truncal ataxia in infancy, telangiectasias, recurrent respiratory infxns → bronchiectasis** • Pts should avoid radiation due to very high risk of lymphoma and carcinoma • ↓ CD4 and CD8 T cells
Bare Lymphocyte Syndrome	• Lack of Class II MHC prevents positive selection of CD4 T cells in the thymus	• Labs →↓ CD4 T cells in blood, but normal number of CD8 cells

TABLE 5 Combined B and T Lymphocyte Deficiencies

DISEASE	PATHOPHYSIOLOGY	PRESENTATION
Severe Combined Immuno-Deficiency (SCID)	• Due to a variety of metabolic or cytokine receptor defects, these are the classic "bubble boy" patients • Can be autosomal recessive, X-linked, or sporadic	• **Viral, bacterial, fungal, and protozoal infections, children get sick within weeks of birth** • Bone marrow transplantation has met with moderate success • Blood transfusions can cause Graft Versus Host Disease (GHVD)
Wiskott-Aldrich Syndrome	• X-linked recessive defect in IgM production to capsular polysaccharides • Also poorly characterized T cell defects	• QUIG →↓ IgM, Nml IgG, ↑ **IgA and IgE**, B cell # normal, T cells anergic • **Classic Triad: eczema, pyogenic bacterial infections, and thrombocytopenia, always in males** • Leukemia and lymphoma is common in children who survive to 10 years old • First line Tx is BMT, second line is IVIG

TABLE 6 Phagocyte Deficiencies

- **Recurrent bacterial infections, usually catalase ⊕(e.g., *Staph*), also *Aspergillus***

DISEASE	PATHOPHYSIOLOGY	PRESENTATION
Chronic Granulomatous Disease	• Phagocytes lack respiratory burst, can engulf microbes but are unable to kill them	• Lab → defective O_2^-/H_2O_2 production by phagocytes • Tx = Recombinant IFN-γ
Leukocyte Adhesion Deficiency Syndromes	• Type I due to lack of β2-integrins (LFA-1) • Type II due to lack of selectin receptors	• **Gingivitis, poor wound healing, and delayed umbilical cord separation** caused because neutrophils can' t extravasate into tissues
Chediak-Higashi Syndrome	• Autosomal recessive defect of microtubule function of neutrophils → inability to fuse lysosome and phagosome	• Present with recurrent infections with *Staph* and *Strep*, **albinism**, peripheral and cranial neuropathies • Lab: giant granules seen in PMN on blood smear
Job' s Syndrome (Hyper-IgE)	• High IgE levels and inhibition of neutrophil chemotaxis	• **"Cold"** ***Staph*** **abscesses** and respiratory infections, **double rows of teeth** in jaw, brittle bones, **classic "gargoyle facies"** • Lab: IgE >2,000 mg/dl (Nml <500)

TABLE 7 Complement Deficiencies

DISEASE	PATHOPHYSIOLOGY	PRESENTATION
Hereditary Angioedema	• Deficiency of C1 esterase inhibitor, so C1 continues to generate vasocative C3a and C5a, causing ↑ capillary permeability and edema	• Brawny edema of face and mouth, and **if edema of supraglottis occurs this can cause fatal airway obstruction** • Tx = ↑ C1 inhibitor concentration with Danazol, or ↓ C1 activation with ε–amino-caproic acid (inhibits plasminogen) • Airway observation
C1, C2, or C4 Deficiency	• Defect in clearance of antigen/antibody complexes	• Present with lupus-like autoimmune disorder, also pyogenic infxn in some
C3 or C5 Deficiency	• Blocks both alternative and classical complement pathways	• Recurrent pyogenic bacterial infections, typically *Staphylococcus*
C6, C7, C8, or C9 Deficiency	• Blocks development of Membrane Attack Complex	• **Classic presentation is recurrent *Neisseria* infections** • Recrudescent *N. meningitidis* meningitis is highly suggestive

B. Acquired Immunodeficiency Syndrome (AIDS)

1. Epidemiology

   a. AIDS is a global pandemic (currently the fastest spread is in southeast Asia and central Europe, Africa is saturated and contains by far the highest prevalence in the world)

   b. **Heterosexual transmission is most common mode worldwide**

   c. In the U.S., IV drug users and their sex partners are the fastest growing population of HIV⊕ patients

   d. Homosexual transmission has stabilized but is still high in the U.S.

2. HIV biology

   a. HIV is a retrovirus with the usual *gag*, *pol*, and *env* genes

   b. p24 is a core protein encoded by *gag* gene, and can be used clinically to follow disease progression

   c. gp120 and gp41 are envelope glycoproteins that are produced on cleavage of gp160, coded by *env*

   d. Reverse Transcriptase (coded by *pol*) converts viral RNA to DNA so it can integrate into the host's DNA

   e. Cellular entry via binding to both CD4 and an additional ligand that is a cytokine receptor (can be CXCR4, CCR5, others)

   f. HIV can infect CD4+ T cells, macrophages, thymic cells, astrocytes, dendritic cells, and others

   g. Mechanisms of CD4 cell destruction are not well understood, but probably include direct cell lysis, induction of CD8+ cytotoxic T lymphocyte responses against infected CD4+ cells, and exhaustion of bone marrow production (suppression of production of T cells)

   h. In addition, the virus induces alterations in host cytokine patterns rendering surviving lymphocytes ineffective

3. Disease Course

   a. In most patients AIDS is relentlessly progressive, and death occurs within 10 to 15 years of HIV infection

   b. Long Term Survivors

      1) **Up to 5% of pts are "Long Term Survivors," meaning the disease does not progress even after 15 to 20 years without Tx**

2) This may be due to infection with defective virus, a potent host immune response, or genetic resistance of the host

3) **People with homozygous CCR5 deletions are highly resistant to HIV infection, and heterozygotes are less resistant**

c. **Although patients can have no clinical evidence of disease for many years, HIV HAS NO LATENT PHASE; clinical silence in those patients who eventually progress is due to daily, temporarily successful host repopulation of T cells**

d. Death is usually caused by opportunistic infections (OIs)

1) OIs typically onset after CD4 counts fall below 200

2) Below 200 CD4 cells, all pts should receive Bactrim prophylaxis against *Pneumocystis carinii* pneumonia (PCP) and *Toxoplasma*

3) Below 50 CD4 cells, all pts should receive azithromycin prophylaxis against *Mycobacterium avium-intracellulare* Complex (MAC)

4) Kaposi's Sarcoma = common skin cancer found in homosexual HIV patients, thought to be caused by co-transmission of Human Herpes Virus 8 (HHV 8)

5) Other diseases found in AIDS patients include generalized wasting, dementia, and high grade B cell lymphomas (risk of lymphoma 100× higher in AIDS pts)

6) Pts also are at higher risk for common infections. For example, there is a logarithmic increase in the risk of *Streptococcus pneumonia*

4. Treatment

a. **HAART** = Highly Active Anti-Retroviral Therapy

1) Cocktail includes 3–4 drug mix of nucleoside analogues (e.g., AZT, ddI, d4T) and protease inhibitors

2) Protease inhibitors block the splicing of the large *gag* precursor protein into its final components, p24 and p7

3) Newest addition to arsenal is hydroxyurea

a) Inhibits host ribonucleotide reductase → decreased concentration of purines

b) ddI is a purine analogue (competitor), so hydroxyurea ↑ efficacy of ddI

c) In theory, virus should not be able to become resistant to hydroxyurea, since it acts on a host enzyme and not on the virus

b. **No patient should ever be on any single drug for HIV—resistance is invariable in monotherapy**

c. Current treatment is able to suppress viral replication to below detectable limits in the majority of patients

d. Failure of the regimen is associated with poor compliance (missed doses lead to resistance) and prior exposure to one or more drugs in the regimen (the virus is already resistant to the agent)

e. The long-term significance of viral suppression is unclear, but it is known that the virus is NOT cleared from the body at up to two years after it ceases to be detectable in the blood (it can be found latent in lymph nodes)

VIII. TESTABLE LABORATORY IMMUNOLOGY

A. Mitogens

1. Mitogens are inducers of mitosis (mitosis + genic = mitogen)
2. Exposure of immune cells to mitogens induces their activation in a polyclonal fashion—that is, all B cells exposed to a B cell mitogen are activated irrespective of their particular antigen specificity
3. Exam questions might name a mitogen and expect you to be able to identify which cell type responds to it (see Table 8)

B. Enzyme-Linked Immunosorbent Assay (ELISA)

1. Used to measure the amount of antigen or antibody in solution
2. ELISAs use antibody chemically linked to a color-generating enzyme to measure the quantity of antigen or antibody in solution
3. Direct ELISA detects the concentration of antigen in solution

a. An antibody directed against the antigen of interest is adsorbed onto a plastic plate

TABLE 8 Mitogens

MITOGEN	AFFECTED CELL
Lipopolysaccharide	B cell only
Concanavalin A (con A)	T cell only
Phytohemagglutinin (PHA)	T cell only
Pokeweed Mitogen (PWM)	B and T cells
Superantigens*	T cell only

* Superantigens are toxins that bind non-specifically to T-cell receptors outside the normal antigen-binding cleft, allowing activation of up to 1/5 of all the T cells in the body at any one time.

b. A solution containing the antigen of interest is poured onto the plate and incubated, allowing binding of the antigen to the antibody

c. A second antibody directed against a different epitope on the antigen is linked to a color-generating enzyme, and then added to the plate

d. After adding the enzymes substrate, the optical density of color generated in the plate can be used to measure the concentration of enzyme present, and thus the concentration of antigen present

4. The indirect ELISA is used to measure the concentration of antibody in serum (this is, for example, the type of ELISA which detects anti-HIV antibodies in human serum)

   a. Antigen to which the antibody of interest binds is adsorbed onto a plastic plate (e.g., to assay for anti-HIV antibodies, HIV proteins are adsorbed onto a plate)

   b. Serum is poured onto the plate and incubated, allowing binding of the antibody of interest to the adsorbed antigen

   c. An enzyme-linked anti-antibody antibody, which binds to the constant region of all IgG molecules, is added to the plate

   d. After adding the enzyme substrate, the concentration of antibody present on the plate can be estimated by measuring the color density generated by the enzyme

C. Western Blot

1. A group of proteins (or serum) is electrophoretically run out on a polyacrylamide gel (PAGE)
2. An antibody that recognizes the protein of interest is tagged with an enzyme that generates a visible color, or with a radiation label, and is added to the gel
3. The presence of the protein of interest is inferred from the generation of a colored line or a radioactive signal on the gel at the right molecular weight for the protein of interest
4. The Western Blot is technically more demanding than the ELISA, but in certain circumstances is more accurate
5. For this reason, in AIDS testing all positive ELISAs are confirmed by Western Blotting

D. Monoclonal Antibodies

1. Repeated immunizations in mice cause the generation of memory B lymphocytes, which generate antibody against the antigen used
2. The spleen of the immunized mouse is removed and B cells are isolated
3. The B cells are mixed with immortal myeloma cells that do not secrete antibody, and the two cell types are induced to fuse together by addition of a special chemical—this generates a hybridoma, a cell containing the chromosomes of both the B lymphocyte and the myeloma cell
4. The hybridomas are grown in a special medium that poisons unfused cells so they cannot grow
5. The hybridomas are thus selected to grow out, and after separating into individual wells, their supernatants can be assayed for the presence of a desired antibody
6. In this way, an immortal hybridoma is generated that produces an antibody of a single specificity, and can be used to generate an unlimited amount of that antibody

REVIEW QUESTIONS

1. Which of the following is the fundamental function of antibody-dependent cell-mediated cytotoxicity (ADCC)?
   a) Antibody directly kills foreign microbes
   b) Antibody attaches to the B cell surface, causing the B cell to undergo apoptosis
   c) The Fc portion of antibody attaches to the T cell surface, and the variable portion provides specificity to T cell-mediated killing
   d) The Fc portion of antibody attaches to the phagocytic cell surface, and the variable portion provides specificity to phagocyte-mediated killing
   e) Antibody directly kills host lymphocytes
2. Which of the following is **not** considered part of the differential diagnosis of eosinophilia?
   a) Infection caused by *Coccidioides immitis*
   b) Infection caused by *Candida albicans*
   c) Infection caused by *Trichinella*
   d) Non-Hodgkin's lymphoma
   e) Systemic lupus erythematosis
3. Which of the following cell types do **not** express Class II MHC molecules?
   a) Macrophages
   b) B lymphocytes
   c) Dendritic cells
   d) T lymphocytes
   e) Endothelial cells
4. An antibody is composed of . . .
   a) 2 heavy chains and 2 light chains.
   b) 2 heavy chains and 1 light chain.
   c) 4 heavy chains and 1 light chain.
   d) 4 heavy chains and 2 light chains.
   e) 4 heavy chains and 4 light chains.

5. Match the following classes of antibody with their functions:

1) IgM	a) Involved in allergic reactions
2) IgD	b) A cell surface receptor with no known immunologic function
3) IgG	c) Protects mucosal surfaces
4) IgE	d) The first antibody produced during an immune response
5) IgA	e) Crosses the placenta

6. Which of the following Ig subtypes can form multimers in serum?
   a) IgM
   b) IgG
   c) IgA
   d) IgM and IgG
   e) IgM and IgA

7. The specificity of antibody is determined by . . .
   a) the Fc domain.
   b) the variable region of the heavy chain.
   c) the flexibility of the hinge region.
   d) the three-dimensional structure formed by the variable region of both the light and heavy chain.
   e) the variable region of the light chain.

8. Match the process to its effect:

1) allelic exclusion	a) Changing surface bound antibody to secreted antibody
2) genetic recombination	b) ↑ antibody binding specificity during B cell proliferation
3) alternative splicing	c) Each B cell expresses antibody of one specificity
4) class switching	d) The generation of antibody specificity
5) affinity maturation	e) Changing from IgM to IgG expression

9. Which of the following accurately describes the CD4 protein?

    a) CD4 is expressed on cytotoxic T cells, and binds to Class I MHC molecules

    b) CD4 is expressed on helper T cells, and binds to Class II MHC molecules

    c) CD4 is expressed on helper T cells, and binds to Class I MHC molecules

    d) CD4 is expressed on cytotoxic T cells, and binds to Class II MHC molecules

    e) CD4 is expressed on natural killer cells, and binds to Class I MHC molecules

10. Which of the following correctly describes the Th1/Th2 paradigm?

    a) Th1 cells secrete IL-4 and protect against parasites, whereas Th2 cells secrete IFN-γ and protect against intracellular infections

    b) Th1 cells secrete IFN-γ and protect against intracellular infections, whereas Th2 cells secrete IL-4 and protect against parasites

    c) Th1 cells secrete IL-4 and protect against intracellular infections, whereas Th2 cells secrete IFN-γ and protect against parasites

    d) Th1 cells secrete IFN-γ and protect against parasites, whereas Th2 cells secrete IL-4 and protect against intracellular infections

    e) Th1 cells secrete IL-4 and protect against parasites, whereas Th2 cells secrete IL-10 and protect against intracellular infections

11. Which of the following correctly describes Class I and Class II MHC molecules?

    a) Class I presents intracellular antigens to CD8 cells; Class II presents extracellular antigens to CD4 cells

    b) Class I presents extracellular antigens to CD8 cells; Class II presents intracellular antigens to CD4 cells

    c) Class I presents extracellular antigens to CD4 cells; Class II presents extracellular antigens to CD8 cells

    d) Both Class I and Class II present intracellular antigens to either CD4 or CD8 cells

e) Neither Class I or Class II is capable of presenting intracellular antigens

12. How are phagocytes recruited to the location of an infection?

a) The brain sends out neurohormones to signal the location

b) Phagocytes randomly leave the vasculature, and some happen to the area of infection by chance

c) Phagocytes are summoned by chemotactic cytokines called chemokines, which are released by damaged cells and cells exposed to damaged host proteins

d) Phagocytes are produced locally at the site of infection by proliferation of macrophages

e) Phagocytes are recruited by antibodies

13. Match the following steps of extravasation to the cell-surface adhesins which mediate them:

1) Rolling	a) PECAM
2) Sticking	b) Selectins
3) Diapedesis	c) ICAM

14. Which of the following statements is true?

a) Innate immune cells possess memory and specificity

b) Adaptive immune cells possess memory and specificity

c) Innate immune cells possess memory, while adaptive immune cells possess specificity

d) Innate immune cells possess specificity, while adaptive immune cells possess memory

e) Both innate and adaptive immune cells possess memory and specificity

15. Which of the following statements regarding tolerance is true?

a) Central tolerance is 100% effective

b) Tolerance is mediated by antibodies

c) Peripheral tolerance is strictly due to cryptic antigens

d) Peripheral tolerance is an important back-up for central tolerance, which is imperfect

e) Peripheral tolerance is strictly due to co-stimulation requirements

16. Match the following cytokines with their most important function:

1) IL-1	a) Endogenous pyrogen
2) IL-2	b) Immunosuppressive
3) IL-4	c) Stimulates phagocytic activity/inflammation
4) IL-10	d) T cell activation
5) IFN-γ	e) Stimulates antibody production

17. Affinity maturation and class switching occur in which microanatomical site?

    a) Parafollicular areas of lymph nodes

    b) Bone marrow

    c) Mucosa

    d) Germinal centers in lymph node follicles

    e) Vascular compartment

18. Match the following types of immunodeficiencies with their key identifying characteristic:

1) Primary B cell deficiencies	a) Encapsulated bacterial infections starting in the teens
2) Primary T cell deficiencies	b) Gingival dz, delayed umbilical cord separation, chronic abscesses
3) Phagocyte deficiencies	c) Viral and bacterial infections starting as a neonate
4) Complement deficiencies	d) Encapsulated bacterial infections starting at 6 months
5) Acquired B cell deficiency	e) Recurrent meningitis

19. Answer True or False to the following questions regarding AIDS:

    a) Homosexual transmission is the most common mode of HIV transmission worldwide.

    b) CD4 is sufficient for viral entry into T cells.

    c) HIV infection is 100% fatal without treatment.

    d) HIV is latent during the asymptomatic phase.

e) The risk of opportunistic infections markedly increases when the CD4 count drops below 200.

f) Homosexual HIV patients are more likely to develop Kaposi's Sarcoma.

g) HIV patients can be effectively treated with two drugs.

h) HIV can be cured in some people by highly active anti-retroviral therapy (HAART).

ANSWERS

1. **d)** Antibody-dependent cell mediated cytotoxicity (ADCC) occurs when the constant region (Fc) of antibody binds to a phagocyte, and the non-specific phagocyte uses the variable portion of the antibody to provide specificity to recognize foreign microbes. This allows targeted digestion of the microbe, while sparing host tissues of the phagocyte's toxic molecules. In this instance, the antibody is only used by the phagocyte to recognize the microbe, and the antibody itself does not mediate any direct killing effect. ADCC is not used by lymphocytes, which are inherently specific due to their variable receptors.
2. **b)** Infections involving multicellular parasites (e.g., worms) typically cause eosinophilia if they are tissue invasive. Thus, organisms that are purely found in the gastrointestinal tract may not cause eosinophilia. *Trichinella*, the causative agent of trichinosis, widely invades parenchymal tissues, and causes a high grade eosinophilia. Neoplasms, particularly those involving white blood cells (leukemia and lymphoma), and any collagen-vascular disease leading to vasculitis also cause eosinophilia. For reasons that are not clear, *Coccidioides immitis* and *Aspergillus* fungal infections can cause eosinophilia, while eosinophilia is not typically seen in *Candida* infections.
3. **d)** Class II MHC (unlike Class I MHC, which is expressed on almost all nucleated cells) is only expressed on "professional antigen presenting cells." Professional antigen presenting cells are those that have two important properties: 1) they are phagocytic and 2) they express co-stimulatory molecules to activate T cells. Macrophages, B cells, and dendritic cells are the classical antigen presenting cells. Interestingly, when stimulated by interferon-γ, endothelial cells can present

antigen via Class II MHC to T cells. T cells, on the other hand, do not present antigen to themselves, and are not antigen presenting cells.

4. **a)** An antibody is a tetramer, and can be thought of as a "dimer of dimers." Its subunit is one heavy chain bound to one light chain (a dimer), and two of these subunits comprise the final molecule (a dimer of the dimers).

5. **1-d, 2-b, 3-e, 4-a, 5-c.** Obviously the various Ig subclasses have multiple different functions, but those listed are the ones most important to remember for exams. IgM is always the first subclass produced. IgD has no known function other than as a surface receptor. IgG crosses the placenta, and is the mainstay of mature immune responses. IgE causes allergic reactions by cross-linking basophils and mast cells, and also is important in protection against worms. IgA is secreted across mucosal surfaces to protect them from external invaders.

6. **e)** IgM tends to form pentamers in serum, as the J chain connects 5 IgM molecules together by their Fc regions. IgA forms dimers by connection via a different J chain. IgG is always monomeric in serum.

7. **d)** The antigen-binding cleft is a three-dimensional surface comprising the intertwined variable regions of the light and heavy chains. The Fc region determines the subclass of Ig (e.g., IgM, IgD, IgG, etc.), but has nothing to do with antigen binding. The hinge region allows flexibility in the antibody, and also has nothing to do with antigen binding.

8. **1-c, 2-d, 3-a, 4-e, 5-b.** Allelic exclusion occurs when a B cell successfully rearranges a heavy chain and light chain allele, preventing any further rearrangements. This means the B cell can only express one type of heavy chain and light chain. Genetic recombination is the mechanism by which alleles are rearranged. Germ-line DNA is recombined to allow variable (V), diversity (D), and joining (J) gene segments to come together to form one V-D-J heavy chain allele, and V-J segments are combined to form one V-J light chain allele. Alternative splicing of messenger RNA can allow either inclusion or exclusion of the transmembrane domain of the coding region. Inclusion causes the mRNA to code for a surface bound protein while exclusion allows coding for a secreted protein. Class switching is the change from an IgM antibody of a given specificity to an IgG antibody of the same specificity. Affinity maturation is a natural selective process in which B cells expressing antibodies with higher

affinities to the stimulating antigen are given survival signals. The result is that during an immune response, the affinity of generated antibody gets progressively higher.

9. **b)** The CD4 protein is a marker for helper T cells. It binds to Class II MHC molecules, thereby stabilizing the interaction between Class II MHC and the T cell receptor. The CD8 protein is a marker for cytotoxic T cells, and binds to Class I MHC molecules.

10. **b)** Th1 cells secrete high levels of IFN-γ, but do not secrete IL-4. IFN-γ stimulates phagocytic activity and inflammation, perfect for protection against intracellular pathogens. Th2 cells secrete high levels of IL-4, but do not secrete IFN-γ. IL-4 stimulates antibody production, and class switching to IgE, perfect for defense against parasites.

11. **a)** Intracellular, cytoplasmic antigens are pumped into the endoplasmic reticulum by the TAP complex, where such antigens bind to Class I MHC molecules. Class I MHC molecules present these cytoplasmic antigens to CD8 cells. Extracellular antigens, taken up by phagocytosis, bind to Class II MHC molecules in the phagolysosomes, and Class II MHC molecules present such antigens to CD4 cells.

12. **c)** Chemotactic cytokines, called chemokines, diffuse into the vascular compartment from their source in tissue exposed to trauma or infection. Such chemokines are secreted either by damaged cells themselves, or are secreted by neighboring cells alerted to the damage by exposure to host proteins leaked by the damaged cells. The chemokines set up a concentration gradient in the nearby vasculature, forming a sort of yellow-brick road that the phagocytes follow back to its source. Antibodies and neurohormones are not directly involved in this recruitment. Macrophages are end-differentiated cells, and are not capable of cell division.

13. **1-b, 2-c, 3-a.** Rolling is caused by the loose binding of selectins on the endothelial cells to selectin receptors on the leukocyte. Sticking is due to a firmer attachment of ICAM on the endothelial cells to one of several ICAM receptors on the leukocyte. Diapedesis is the process by which the leukocyte squeezes in between neighboring endothelial cells, and binds to the molecule PECAM at the endothelial junction, using PECAM to pull itself across the endothelial monolayer.

14. **b)** Only adaptive immune cells (i.e., lymphocytes) possess memory and specificity. Innate immune cells (i.e., phagocytes) are non-specific and react to a given antigen in the same manner no matter how often they have been exposed

to that antigen before. Memory allows lymphocytes to become more avid for a given antigen (affinity maturation), and to respond more quickly and with a more potent response with each successive exposure to the antigen.

15. **d)** Central tolerance involves deletion of auto-reactive T cells in the thymus. Since not all host antigens are expressed in the thymus, central tolerance cannot possibly tolerize T cells to all the different antigens in the host. Therefore, peripheral tolerance is an absolutely required fail-safe to prevent autoimmunity. Peripheral tolerance occurs outside of the thymus. Three main mechanisms cause peripheral tolerance. First, antigenic ignorance is the sequestration of host antigens from lymphocytes. If lymphocytes never see a given host antigen, none can ever become reactive to it. Second, recognition of antigen is not enough for a T cell to be turned on. Instead, the antigen-presenting cell must co-stimulate the T cell by expressing a second stimulating marker. Antigen-presenting cells only express these second signals when the antigen-presenting cells have been exposed to some danger signal in the environment (e.g., microbial fractions or inflammatory cytokines). Finally, we do not mount reactions to foodstuffs because TGF-β in the gut tolerizes T cells to gastrointestinal antigens (so-called oral tolerance).

16. **1-a, 2-d, 3-e, 4-b, 5-c.** IL-1 is synthesized by most human cell types and released upon damage to the cell (it is thus a danger signal). It directly stimulates the fever response in the hypothalamus. IL-2 is the *sine qua non* for T cell proliferation; when you think IL-2, think T cells. IL-4 is a key cytokine for stimulating antibody production; when you think IL-4, think antibodies. IL-10 is probably the most immunosuppressive cytokine known. It shuts down expression of almost every cytokine, including itself, and inhibits inflammation. IFN-γ is crucial to stimulating phagocytes to uptake and kill microbes.

17. **d)** The germinal centers of lymph node follicles are the sites of massive B cell proliferation following activation by antigen. During this proliferation, the lymphoblasts undergo a million-fold increase in the mutation rate only at the Ig loci (remarkably, the mutation rate does not increase elsewhere in the genome). The presence of antigen which continues to select for high affinity B cell receptor binding, combined with an environment of rapid mutation, leads to Darwinian evolution of the B cells in the germinal center. Thus, only those B cells whose Ig mutations lead to higher affinity binding are selected to continue to grow. The result is affinity

maturation. Class switching also occurs here due to T cell help provided by CD40-ligand binding to CD40 on the B cells.

18. **1-d, 2-c, 3-b, 4-e, 5-a.** Phenotypes in patients with primary B cell deficiencies do not appear until maternal IgG is cleared from the newborn child's serum. This process takes about six months, so with good clinical reliability (and 100% reliability on standardized exams), primary B cell deficiencies present AT AGE 6 MONTHS! B cell defects allow infections by encapsulated bacteria (e.g., *Hemophilus, Streptococcus, E. coli,* etc). Conversely, T cell deficiencies allow infections by both viruses and bacteria (as well as fungi), but these present within weeks of birth, allowing an easy time-course differentiation from B cell defects. Phagocyte deficiencies allow a variety of infections but clinically the lack of phagocytes prevents easy separation of the umbilical cord (phagocytes chew off the cord by secreting lytic enzymes), allow terrible gingival disease to set in, and prevent the resolution of simple skin and subcutaneous infections, causing chronic abscesses. There are many different kinds of complement deficiencies; however, the most famous (and most testable) are deficiencies in components of the membrane attack complex (MAC). MAC is crucial to protection against *Neisseria*, so these patients get recurrent *N. meningitidis* meningitis. In fact, *N. meningitidis* is so susceptible to antibiotics that any patient who fails therapy and recrudesces should immediately be screened for complement deficiencies. Acquired B cell defect refers to common variable hypogammaglobulinemia, a defect whose pathogenesis is not understood. This presents with encapsulated bacterial infections starting any time between the teen years to young adulthood.

19. **a) False**—heterosexual is most common worldwide

    b) False—along with CD4, a co-receptor such as CCR5 or CXCR4 are needed for viral entry

    c) False—about 5% of HIV infected patients are Long Term Non-progressors, who never get sick for unclear reasons

    d) False—HIV has no latent phase in its life-cycle, the asymptomatic period is due to immune reconstitution keeping pace with HIV-mediated T cell destruction

    e) True—this is why all patients with CD4 counts below 200 should be started on Bactrim prophylaxis

    f) True—Kaposi's Sarcoma is due to co-infection with Human

Herpes Virus 8, which is more commonly transmitted during homosexual sex, thus it is in fact important in a sick HIV patient to find out how he or she acquired the disease, because the differential diagnosis of opportunistic infections differs somewhat depending upon the route of HIV transmission

g) False—standard of care is three or more anti-retrovirals

h) False—although the virus can be suppressed below the limit of detectability in the majority of patients, there is NO EVIDENCE that these patients are cured, and indeed when investigators have stopped drug therapy after several years of total suppression, the virus has invariably repopulated itself from latent reservoirs in the lymph system. (Although some investigators think cure might be possible if suppression is maintained for long enough to allow memory T cells, which harbor the virus, to die—this might require 30 years or more of therapy!)

INDEX

Page numbers followed by *f* refer to figures; those followed by *t* refer to tables.

A